NEW DIRECTIONS FOR MENTAL HEALTH SERVICES

H. Richard Lamb, *University of Southern California*
EDITOR-IN-CHIEF

D1231046

Managed Behavioral Health Care: Current Realities and Future Potential

David Mechanic
Rutgers University

EDITOR

Number 78, Summer 1998

JOSSEY-BASS PUBLISHERS
San Francisco

MANAGED BEHAVIORAL HEALTH CARE: CURRENT REALITIES AND FUTURE POTENTIAL
David Mechanic (ed.)
New Directions for Mental Health Services, no. 78
H. Richard Lamb, Editor-in-Chief

Microfilm copies of issues and articles are available in 16mm and 35mm, as well as microfiche in 105mm, through University Microfilms Inc., 300 North Zeeb Road, Ann Arbor, Michigan 48106–1346.

ISSN 0193-9416   ISBN 0-7879-1429-0

NEW DIRECTIONS FOR MENTAL HEALTH SERVICES is part of The Jossey-Bass Psychology Series and is published quarterly by Jossey-Bass Inc., Publishers, 350 Sansome Street, San Francisco, California 94104–1342.

SUBSCRIPTIONS cost $63.00 for individuals and $105.00 for institutions, agencies, and libraries.

EDITORIAL CORRESPONDENCE should be sent to the Editor-in-Chief, H. Richard Lamb, University of Southern California, Department of Psychiatry, Graduate Hall, 1937 Hospital Place, Los Angeles, California 90033–1071.

Cover photograph by Wernher Krutein/PHOTOVAULT © 1990.

Jossey-Bass Web address: www.josseybass.com

Printed in the United States of America on acid-free recycled paper containing 100 percent recovered waste paper, of which at least 20 percent is postconsumer waste.

CONTENTS

Editor's Notes

Five years ago no one would have predicted how substantially behavioral health care would grow, its coverage of most of the American population, and the rapidity with which it would change health care networks, mental health practices, and the fortunes and conditions of work of mental health professionals. The behavioral health care industry remains an industry in flux, one characterized by mergers and realignments and growth of large firms dominating the marketplace. After achieving a foothold in the private insurance sector, behavioral health is now moving rapidly into the public sector and beginning to involve some of our most vulnerable clients.

Behavioral health care is developing in an increasingly acrimonious context. Mental health professionals faced with major pressures to modify professional practices are often harsh and vociferous critics. Consumers and their advocates, fearful that needed services will be limited or withheld, have also been highly critical. Media give attention to some of the most blatant abuses, spreading the impression that managed care companies are primarily concerned with profits and not with patients' welfare. Politicians find managed care a popular and easy target, and hundreds of bills are introduced each year in state legislatures and Congress to regulate its practice. There is much confusion, discomfort, and uncertainty in this arena.

Our challenge is not to damn or praise behavioral health care but rather to better understand how it is functioning and how it can be shaped to perform more adequately. Behavioral health companies did not develop in a vacuum. They grew in response to the need of purchasers to achieve cost containment and more cost-effective care. Consumers complain that behavioral health care companies do not provide needed services. Behavioral health care executives claim, in turn, that they are prepared to provide whatever care purchasers and the public at large are prepared to pay for. Legislators aware of the growing disquiet often assert themselves, sometimes in meaningless and damaging ways. The purpose of this sourcebook is to describe the developing arena of managed care more carefully and provide guidance as to how it might be better shaped in the years ahead.

In Chapter One, I describe the context of managed care, the risks and opportunities it presents, and some of the dilemmas we face as we look ahead, particularly in relation to people with the most serious and persistent mental illnesses. In Chapter Two, Marsha Gold provides the most recent data available that describe the complexity of managed care and the diversity of arrangements that managed care companies make with purchasers and providers. Richard C. Surles and Robert J. Fox follow with an industry perspective and seek to convey that the breadth and quality of services depend on societal values and purchaser decisions as much as on behavioral health care practices. In Chapter

Four, Mark Schlesinger describes trends in utilization review and makes a strong case for the importance of developing mechanisms to build and support advocacy for patient needs. This section of the sourcebook then concludes with a chapter by Richard G. Frank and Thomas G. McGuire on some of the complexities of behavioral health care carve-outs.

The sourcebook then turns to a variety of special issues. In Chapter Six, Robert E. Hurley and Debra A. Draper describe developments in Medicaid managed care and alert us to important issues and difficulties managed care companies face as they become more involved in serving some of America's most vulnerable populations. In Chapter Seven, Kathleen N. Lohr, William E. Schlenger, and J. William Luckey present the logic of quality assurance and indicate some of the difficulties of extending quality measures and activities to the mental health and substance abuse managed care areas. In Chapter Eight, Laura Lee Hall and Richard Beinecke present data from a survey carried out by the National Alliance for the Mentally Ill on the perceptions, experiences, and concerns of consumers about behavioral health practices. This is followed by a chapter by Sara Rosenbaum on the importance of skillful contracting and some of the issues and complexities in contract law that are likely to affect clients.

The third section of the sourcebook presents three case evaluations of states that have moved vulnerable Medicaid clients into managed care. In Chapter Ten, Nicole Lurie and her colleagues examine the longest ongoing study, in Utah, tracing how managed care affected the practice of CMHCs and patient outcomes of varying kinds. In Chapter Eleven, Jaclyn W. Hausman, Neal Wallace, and Joan R. Bloom describe early experience in Colorado's efforts to introduce managed care for its mentally ill Medicaid clients. In Chapter Twelve, Barbara Dickey and her colleagues use Massachusetts data to examine the impact of managed care on utilization and cost of care for mentally ill Medicaid enrollees. These cases convey the variety of managed care structures and arrangements, the complexities of carrying out careful evaluative studies, and the importance of carefully specifying varying kinds of outcomes and follow-up periods. Varying subgroups experience managed care differently and effects change over time. In the last section, I conclude the sourcebook with some observations about the future of managed care.

It is worth emphasizing again the key point of this sourcebook. Discussions of managed care are dominated by emotion and rhetoric and failure to differentiate among the varying structures, approaches, and strategies that are called managed care. These discussions rarely take account of the complexity of the arena or the failures of mental health systems prior to the introduction of managed care. If we are to shape managed care constructively, we first need clear understanding of how it is structured, how it functions, and when it performs well and poorly. This should help identify how practices can best be monitored, evaluated, and, if necessary, regulated. Hopefully this sourcebook will help readers along this path.

David Mechanic
Editor

DAVID MECHANIC is director of the Institute for Health, Health Care Policy, and Aging Research, and René Dubos University Professor of Behavioral Science, Rutgers University.

PART ONE

The Context of Mental Health Managed Care

Our responsibility is not solely to be critics but to help make managed care more effective and responsive.

The Changing Face of Mental Health Managed Care

David Mechanic

My earlier sourcebook (Mechanic and Aiken, 1989) described the theory of capitation and some of the likely pitfalls in its implementation. A central point of that volume was the enormous gap between theory and reality and the complicated task of organizing capitated mental health organizations to provide high-quality, cost-effective care, especially to persons with severe and persistent mental illness. Almost a decade has passed and mental health managed care has grown enormously. It is estimated that in 1996 more than 140 million people had their behavioral mental health benefits managed (Ross, 1997). Such management covered the entire range from full-service HMOs to utilization management by behavioral health companies, although the latter is the dominant pattern. Despite this rapid growth, large gaps in our knowledge and understanding remain about the quality of mental health services and how managed care practices affect persons with mental illness. There is a great deal of rhetoric and anecdote but little systematic data on performance.

Managed Care Today

Managed care consists of a range of organizational structures, approaches, and strategies that may vary a great deal from one context to another (Mechanic, Schlesinger, and McAlpine, 1995). A great deal depends on the motivations and managerial philosophy of managed care companies, the quality and supervision of their case managers and utilization reviewers, the competence and quality of their professional networks, and the integrity of their treatment protocols. Most managed behavioral health companies are large for-profit organizations that operate across different types of employers and geographic areas.

The industry is dominated by a relatively small number of large firms, and their networks and operations may function differently from one place to another. The newness of managed care, its association with privatization, and the dearth of serious outcome data makes trust a central issue in public perceptions (Mechanic and Schlesinger, 1996).

Many mental health advocates and mental health professionals are suspicious of the motives behind managed care practices and believe that care is likely to be improperly denied or limited to reduce costs and increase profitability. They use anecdotal data and atrocity stories that are readily available to support their claims that managed care is harmful, generalizing to the totality of the managed care industry (Mechanic, 1997b). The managed behavioral health industry in turn is making efforts to develop measures that seek to evaluate behavioral health performance and convey a more positive picture to a distrusting public. In 1994 the industry organized the American Managed Behavioral Health Care Association (AMBHA), which represents seventeen managed behavioral health care organizations covering eighty million people (Ross and Croze, 1997). AMBHA is trying to develop credible, measurable standards to monitor industry effectiveness in the areas of access, consumer satisfaction, and quality of care. In the quality area, for example, standards include such issues as outpatient follow-up of patients with depression discharged from hospital, continuity of care, medication management for patients with schizophrenia, and need for detoxification services in the three-month period after having received such services. Measuring quality is, of course, a complex and tricky process, and such measures are at best only very crude indicators. But they constitute efforts of the behavioral health industry to establish its credibility with a skeptical professional community and a distrusting public.

There is cause to question the goals and priorities of the behavioral health industry, but the motives of professional critics also need to be examined. Managed care is changing professional worlds, professional opportunities, clinical autonomy, and reimbursement. Managed care companies may include or exclude such professionals from care networks, may be tough bargainers over fees and remuneration arrangements, and may put pressure on professionals to change the settings and intensity of their usual treatment practices. In inpatient settings, the payment of discounted hospital rates and pressures to reduce length of stay put increased work demands on clinical and administrative staff, who are themselves facing reductions in force in the quest for more efficient care (Mechanic, 1997a). Professional prospects look less promising than they once were, and this colors the way many mental health professionals see emerging trends.

Savings and Cost Shifting

Although systematic evidence is lacking, all indications are that behavioral health succeeds in reducing mental health costs for employers (Mechanic, Schlesinger, and McAlpine, 1995). While it provides comparable or even improved access to mental health care when compared with the traditional system, it substantially reduces the intensity of care in a way that results in substantial savings. Evidence of savings to employers, however, is not convincing if costs are shifted to patients, their families, or the community. Evidence of such cost shifting is difficult to obtain, though there are some indications of increased patient and family burdens under managed care. This needs to be monitored carefully.

Managed care companies offer their services on an administrative or risk basis. Risk-based contracts—that is, contracts in which the behavioral health company takes responsibility for providing needed mental health services at a capitated rate per enrollee—are becoming more common (Frank, Huskamp, McGuire, and Newhouse, 1996). Managed care is a customized product, and a bewildering array of arrangements and combinations have developed to fit the needs of particular purchasers: employee assistance programs, mental health services, and substance abuse services. These may be joined together or carved out separately. Capitation is commonly used to reimburse primary care physicians in network/IPA HMOs, often combined with withholds and bonuses (Gold and others, 1995). There are no systematic data indicating how mental health professionals are paid by managed care companies. Some capitation is used to reimburse psychiatrists, though the arrangement is much less common than in primary care and in some general specialties like pediatrics. Capitation seems to be little used in paying nonphysician mental health providers thus far, with most payment in the form of discount fee-for-service. Capitation is, however, a common form of payment to staff and group model HMOs, which integrate services for enrollee populations. Many of these HMOs, however, also carve out mental health and substance abuse services in contracts with behavioral health providers.

Managing Care for the Most Vulnerable Populations

More recently, state Medicaid authorities have aggressively moved their Medicaid populations into managed care arrangements, and states are now beginning to extend managed mental health care to its disabled populations as well. These arrangements involve far more impaired and vulnerable patients than those typically found in the employment sector, and shifting these populations to managed care raises complex and difficult issues. Unlike the employment sector, where it seemed evident that careful management of care could readily reduce cost, Medicaid's opportunities for large cost reductions are less evident. Many persons with severe and persistent mental illness were already having their care managed within the public sector and shifting to capitation may not necessarily reduce cost over the long run, though some immediate cost savings seem to occur. Even more uncertain is whether managed care companies have the appropriate orientation and experience to effectively manage the types of complex problems typical of many clients with severe and persistent illness.

Key issues in managed care for persons with severe and persistent illness involve the needed basket of acute care and long-term care services, who is responsible for providing them, their appropriate coordination, and possibilities of shifting costs among sectors. Mental health care as traditionally defined in the acute care psychiatric sector tends to follow a relatively narrow medical definition and does not typically include needed social services, psychosocial rehabilitation, assistance with housing and entitlements, and related issues. A recent study of expenditures for public clients with serious mental illness in Wisconsin (Hollingsworth and Sweeney, 1997) found that a significant proportion of total outlays were for services not usually provided by behavioral health providers. For example, 12 percent of expenditures went for residential services, 8 percent for community support services, and 6 percent for vocational services. Other services typically not provided included transportation, training in daily living skills, supportive home care, and the like. The investigators estimate that more than two-fifths of all expenditures were for broad rehabilitative services. Some of these services are available within managed care programs.

The needs and expenditure patterns for persons with serious mental impairments raise a number of important issues as states move more aggressively into managed care for disabled populations. First, states are not likely to receive expanded services for their disabled populations under managed care unless they specifically contract for them and hold managed care accountable. The need for clarity is particularly important because under law the court's presumption of the correctness of the state's regulatory interpretations shifts in contractual situations. In contract disputes interpretations tend to go against the drafter on the presumption that "the drafter knew what it wanted and had a corresponding duty to draft with clarity" (Rosenbaum, 1997, pp. 194–195). Second, failure to provide appropriate long-term treatment and rehabilitation—whether it be continuity of medication management or assertive community case management—may result in displacement of problems to the social services or criminal justice system. Inadequately managed patients may cause problems in the community, and arrest and incarceration is not uncommon. More subtly, poor community treatment may add to family burdens, endanger clients, and increase their victimization. These shifts in social costs are not typically monitored—but such auditing is essential to a well-functioning system. Even more subtly, patients receiving inadequate services or receiving poorly managed and poorly coordinated care may have less positive opportunities for decent housing, meaningful employment, and a reasonable quality of life.

A troublesome ambiguity involves the role of the public safety net when states and localities contract for mental health services with private vendors. States are moving aggressively into managed care to cut costs and free themselves from organizational and regulatory constraints associated with union contracts, civil service arrangements, and bureaucracy. There is an expectation that the private sector can perform the necessary tasks more easily and in a more cost-effective way. States seeking economies may have little motivation to maintain public programs or subsidize nonprofit and private programs that persons with serious mental illness have depended on for the past twenty years. But if states and localities do not maintain this capacity, what is the fallback when private organizations fail? Among the issues that need careful consideration are the extent to which states should maintain safety net institutions, the extent to which contractors should be required to use essential mental health providers, and the future role of major state institutions such as public mental hospitals, forensic hospitals, and specialized programs.

States, of course, may exclude any population they wish from managed care contracts and until recently persons with severe and persistent mental illness were in that category. But even within the included population, states might exclude persons with long histories of inpatient hospitalization, those with complicated and difficult-to-treat comorbidities, and those judged to be dangerous, as well as forensic cases or other subgroups. States also may require that managed care providers work through existing essential providers and particular public institutions. Contracts, for example, may allow a designated number of inpatient days in public institutions per thousand clients, with managed care contractors responsible for any costs beyond this threshold. Structuring risk between the states and managed care providers is a complicated process, and sharing risk seems to be the preferable approach (Frank, Huskamp, McGuire, and Newhouse, 1996). Generally the approach is to establish risk corridors in a way that motivates judicious use of resources but contains tendencies to reduce quality by seeking large profits. States may also limit in various ways the range of allowable profits and administrative costs.

Capitation and Patient Advocacy

Frank, Huskamp, McGuire, and Newhouse (1996) speculate that managed care carve-outs are an attractive option for purchasers because they limit opportunities for risk selection among health plans and health providers. Risk selection is a particularly challenging issue for mental health and substance abuse because these clients tend to be high users of both medical and mental health and substance abuse services and can be very costly. Moreover, there is presently no adequate risk adjustment that can compensate plans that attract more difficult and costly cases. Indeed, plans that are particularly good at serving complicated cases—and therefore develop a reputation that attracts such clients—are at a distinct disadvantage. The existing incentives are not conducive to high-quality care for such populations. Carve-outs hold a single entity responsible for all mental health services for an enrolled population and avoid perverse selection. The managed care entities must, of course, have procedures in place to limit risk selection among provider groups in their networks.

Although capitation is only used in a limited way to pay providers, managed care companies have considerable power over mental health professionals, particularly in communities where such personnel exist in large numbers. The companies exercise such control by credentialing of network members, aggressive discounting, and utilization and quality reviews. Since managed care firms can in many instances substitute social workers and psychologists for psychiatrists and can control the flow of large numbers of clients, they have considerable leverage in bargaining over fees. The dependence many mental health professionals develop on obtaining patients through participation in managed care networks is potentially troublesome if such personnel refrain from patient advocacy for fear of losing access to patients. The need to develop mechanisms to protect patient advocacy may grow exponentially as managed care penetration grows.

Evaluation of behavioral health managed care is primitive. There are many issues that need to be monitored and understood. We know little about how companies' capacities and scope of network vary and how within the same company they vary from one region to another. We have little information on risk arrangements and the levels of risk transferred to varying levels of managed care. We have little information on how much of the capitation dollar is devoted to direct service delivery and how this compares with more traditional practices. And we know almost nothing about the varying intensity of utilization review beyond the fact that practices vary widely (Schlesinger, Gray, and Perreira, 1997), the way in which practice guidelines are used, and the nature of quality assurance systems in place and how they work.

Advocates, benefit officers, and purchasers need improved process and also outcome measures that allow assessment of managed care performance. Any serious measurement will require appropriate severity adjustments that correct for the fact that different providers take on challenges of varying magnitude. Among the issues to be monitored at the process level are medication continuity and compliance, inpatient-outpatient continuity, rates of rehospitalization, involvement of patients and family in treatment planning, quality of housing placement, substance abuse screening, availability of psychosocial rehabilitation, and whether there is a clear focus of responsibility. Typical outcome measures reported are reduced utilization and cost and patient and family satisfaction. More focus is needed, however, on evidence of clinical status, quality of life, family burden, function in such areas as employment, rates of dangerous events such as assault, suicide, violence and victimization, and arrest and imprisonment. Health plans may not have much control over some of these areas—but unusually poor outcomes are often indicative of problematic care needing intensive investigation.

Managed Care in Historical Context

In examining the claims and performance of managed care critically we must also keep in mind the failures of the traditional system of care. Managed care is an easy target, but many of the criticisms of managed care, and others as well, apply to what has gone before. Mental health services have often been poorly organized, fragmented, and unresponsive. Professional practice has been characterized by little discipline and lack of clear standards of care, and treatment has often been unfocused and wasteful of resources. There has been little supervision or accountability, and often the most resources were invested in those least seriously impaired. Many patients were overtreated while those with greater needs received no treatment at all.

Our task, thus, is not solely to be critics but to devote our energies to making managed care more responsive and more effective. It is worth reiteration that managed care is simply a set of structures and strategies that can be applied in varying ways with different motives and diverse outcomes. At its worst it produces profits for stockholders while eroding the intensity and quality of care. But is also has potential to provide early and responsive access and evaluation, to organize and integrate needed services in a seamless web, to monitor and influence the performance of mental health professionals in constructive ways, to bring a more grounded, evidence-based approach to everyday practice, and to produce a more cost-effective product. We are only at the beginning of this long and sometimes confusing trajectory. But the outcome is in no way inevitable and it remains susceptible to our influence.

References

Frank, R. G., Huskamp, H. A., McGuire, T. G., and Newhouse, J. P. "Some Economics of Mental Health Carve-Outs." *Archives of General Psychiatry,* 1996, *53,* 933–937.

Gold, M. R., Hurley, R., Lake, T., Ensor, T., and Berenson, R. "A National Survey of the Arrangements Managed-Care Plans Make with Physicians." *New England Journal of Medicine,* 1995, *333,* 1678–1683.

Hollingsworth, E. J., and Sweeney, J. K. "Mental Health Expenditures for Services for People with Severe Mental Illness." *Psychiatric Services,* 1997, *48,* 485–490.

Mechanic, D. (ed.). *Improving Inpatient Psychiatric Treatment in an Era of Managed Care.* New Directions for Mental Health Services, no. 73. San Francisco: Jossey-Bass, 1997a.

Mechanic, D. "Managed Care as a Target of Distrust." *Journal of the American Medical Association,* 1997b, *277,* 1810–1811.

Mechanic, D., and Aiken, L. H. (eds.). *Paying for Services: Promises and Pitfalls of Capitation.* New Directions for Mental Health Services, no. 43. San Francisco: Jossey-Bass, 1989.

Mechanic, D., and Schlesinger, M. "The Impact of Managed Care on Patients' Trust in Medical Care and Their Physicians." *Journal of the American Medical Association,* 1996, *275,* 1693–1697.

Mechanic, D., Schlesinger, M., and McAlpine, D. "Management of Mental Health and Substance Abuse Services: State of the Art and Early Results." *Milbank Quarterly,* 1995, *73,* 19–55.

Rosenbaum, S. "Protecting Children: Defining, Measuring, and Enforcing Quality in Managed Care." In R.E.K. Stein (ed.), *Health Care for Children: What's Right, What's Wrong, What's Next.* New York: United Hospital Fund of New York, 1997.

Ross, E. C. "Managed Behavioral Health Care Premises, Accountability Systems of Care, and AMBHA's PERMS." *Evaluation Review,* 1997, *21,* 318–321.

Ross, E. C., and Croze, C. "Mental Health Service Delivery in the Age of Managed Care." In T. R. Watkins and J. W. Callicut (eds.), *Mental Health Policy and Practice Today.* Thousand Oaks, Calif.: Sage, 1997.

Schlesinger, M. J., Gray, B. H., and Perreira, K. M. "Medical Professionalism Under Managed Care: The Pros and Cons of Utilization Review." *Health Affairs,* 1997, *16,* 106–124.

DAVID MECHANIC is director of the Institute for Health, Health Care Policy, and Aging Research and René Dubos University Professor of Behavioral Sciences, Rutgers University.

Arrangements between plans and providers are becoming increasingly complex.

The Managed Care Context: Emerging Practices

Marsha Gold

Health care financing has changed dramatically in the 1990s, spurred to a large extent by changes in the market. Purchasers seek to slow growth in spending within a health care system perceived by many as excessively bloated. Managed care, in such forms as health maintenance organizations (HMOs), preferred provider organizations (PPOs), and hybrid point-of-service (POS) plans, has evolved into the dominant form of coverage for privately insured individuals (Jensen, Morrisey, Gaffney, and Liston, 1997). Growing rapidly in public programs as well, it accounts for over a third of Medicaid beneficiaries and 14 percent of Medicare beneficiaries (Health Care Financing Administration, 1997).

The shift to managed care is occurring in an environment in which market-based approaches to cost control are emphasized. Increasingly, the health care system is taking on a business orientation—symbolized by industry consolidation, the growth of national firms, and an expanding publicly traded, for-profit sector (Corrigan, Eden, Gold, and Pickreign, 1997). Market pressure is creating a corresponding pressure in the traditional nonprofit sector, leading to debate about the potential impact on community benefits (Claxton, Feder, Shactman, and Altman, 1997; Gray, 1997). All these trends have affected providers, an increasing share of whom are affiliated, at least by contract, in an increasingly complex set of organizational and contractual arrangements (Shortell and Hull, 1996).

Note: This chapter was supported in part through Mathematica Policy Research. Pat McCall provided secretarial support and Daryl Hall provided editorial assistance.

Today's behavioral health care companies originated as a response to the rapid growth of private, for-profit psychiatric hospitals in the mid to late 1980s and the associated growth in inpatient utilization (Iglehart, 1996). Originally focused on utilization review and similar mechanisms that would encourage alternatives to expensive inpatient services, managed behavioral health care firms have grown to the point where many are now both highly consolidated and provider affiliated, generating distinct behavioral health care systems. Knowing how behavioral health and managed care systems intersect is critical to understanding how behavioral health care services are provided to various people, many of whom are enrolled in managed care organizations. This chapter provides a framework to aid in doing so, then goes on to discuss emerging practices.

A key assumption behind this analysis is that joint consideration of behavioral health and managed care systems is critical because purchasers are not likely to separate their decisions about how to structure behavioral health services from decisions about how to structure general health benefits. Furthermore, there is great overlap between medical and needs and conditions.

A Framework for Managed Care and Behavioral Health Care Services

Figure 2.1 illustrates the decisions that determine the structure of managed care and behavioral health care services. The framework is best considered from top to bottom. The top half shows both how purchasers define the health insurance products they choose and the incentives faced by those covered in selecting among these options. The bottom half of the figure shows the structure of individual plans in the purchaser's coverage. For network-based managed care plans, this structure reflects the type of provider network, how providers are paid and the incentives this creates, and the processes integral to the delivery of care offered by the plan. Behavioral health care services may be embedded, as other services, in the general delivery system of the plan; they may be provided through a distinct and separate structure; or they may be offered in a hybrid way, involving elements of both approaches. These structures and their influence on the delivery of care are one important influence on the quality and outcomes of care. Such outcomes may be simultaneously influenced by the contracting and regulatory decisions of purchasers and regulators that influence who bears the risk for the cost of health care, the obligations of the purchaser, plan, and provider with regard to setting medical standards, and the mechanisms to oversee quality and utilization management. Unfortunately, we know very little about the effects of these arrangements on the quality of care and patient outcomes.

Current Practices in Managed Care

Current research provides insights on key trends in product design, provider networks, provider payment, and care delivery.

Figure 2.1 Managed Care and Behavioral Health Services: Classifying Arrangements and Influences

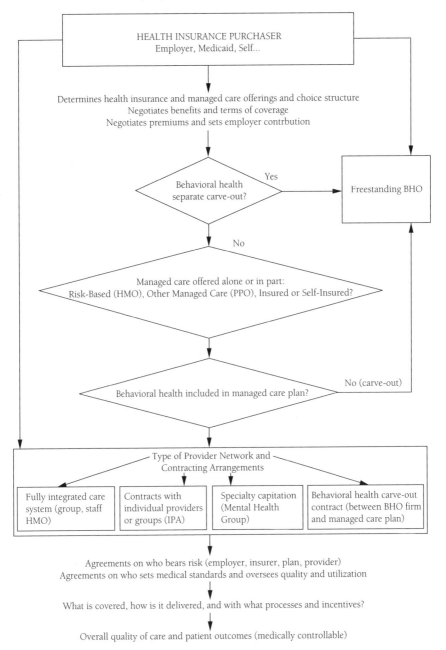

Product Design and Offerings. The range of managed care products is growing more diverse, with many organizations offering multiple products. In a 1994 national survey of HMOs and PPOs, almost three-quarters (71 percent) of plans surveyed offered two or more managed care products, including traditional HMOs, open-ended HMOs, traditional PPOs, gatekeeper PPOs, and exclusive provider organizations (EPOs) (Gold and Hurley, 1997). As the rationale for such growth, plans cited the desire to give consumers a choice and to facilitate the transition to managed care.

Despite the proliferation of products, however, most seem to differ in only a few key dimensions. The main differences involve whether the entity offering a product is at risk for the costs of the product, and whether those selecting the product are locked in to using the providers in the product network (Gold and others, 1995a).

Another key distinguishing feature is the form of the physician practice organization and the extent to which its relationship to the managed care entity is an exclusive one. These features determine whether the network is oriented more toward the traditional staff or group practice type of HMO, or to the now more common network/IPA model. The relationship between product and features, however, has been breaking down. For example, risk—traditionally the defining feature of HMO products—was absent in PPOs and non-HMO POS plans. Under ERISA, however, many employers have self-insured their non-HMO products, and an increasing number want to do the same with their HMO products. As a result, the proportion of HMOs offering self-insured products increased from 25 percent to 65 percent between 1990 and 1994 (American Association of Health Plans, 1996). Conversely, some employers are setting up PPOs as exclusive provider organizations that closely resemble the HMO structure but fall outside state regulations for such products.

The growth and increasing diversity of managed care is reflected in the way purchasers now structure their health benefits. Between 1993 and 1995, the percentage of insured workers nationwide who had a choice between two or more health plans increased from 56 percent to 62 percent, with managed care typically being the new option offered when purchasers moved from one to two products (Jensen, Morrisey, Gaffney, and Liston, 1997). Traditionally the province of larger firms, managed care has become more dominant in the small employer market as well. In 1995, 32 percent of firms with fewer than 49 employees offered only a conventional plan, down from 59 percent in 1993 (Jensen, Morrisey, Gaffney, and Liston, 1997). Even when a single plan is offered, it is now likely to be a managed care plan. In addition, employer-sponsored plans are now more likely to be self-insured. However, this is still least likely for HMOs—only 11 percent of workers enrolled in HMOs were in self-insured plans in 1995 (Jensen, Morrisey, Gaffney, and Liston, 1997). This compares to half or more of workers enrolled in other plans.

Commercial coverage of behavioral health care tends to be restricted, whether in managed care or conventional insurance, with benefits limited and cost sharing more extensive than for other health care services (Buck and Umland, 1997). In

HMOs, for example, mental health benefits typically cover twenty outpatient visits and thirty inpatient days per year; a $20 copayment per outpatient visit is common (American Association of Health Plans, 1996). Furthermore, the emphasis historically has been on an acute care benefit, with coverage often restricted to services appropriate for short-term treatment or crisis intervention (Shadle and Christianson, 1989). In 1990, 46 percent of HMOs excluded treatment for chronic mental illness (Christianson, Wholey, and Peterson, 1997), though plans probably varied in how tightly this was defined. Recent federal legislation to encourage greater parity between mental health and other health care services may change these trends but the effects are likely to be muted by the exclusions and limits built into the legislation (Frank, Koyanagi, and McGuire, 1997).

Provider Network Design. As managed care has expanded to cover a larger geographic base and population, the provider networks associated with managed care plans have become more complex. For example, a 1994 national survey of HMOs and PPOs shows that over half the plans (53 percent) contracted with physicians both directly and through "intermediate entities," while only 33 percent contracted *just* with individual physicians (Gold and others, 1995b). Of the plans that contracted with intermediate entities, 92 percent had a contract with one or more large groups of physicians; 71 percent, with one or more IPAs; 32 percent, with one or more physician-hospital organizations (PHOs); and 26 percent had "other arrangements." Even group and staff model HMOs, which originated as integrated prepaid group practices, reported that one-third or more of the care they provide is delivered by medical practices with fewer than sixteen physicians. Half the group and staff model plans (51 percent) reported that their traditional HMO product is delivered through a mixed model that includes elements of network/IPA arrangements. Other studies have also found evidence for this kind of complexity (InterStudy, 1997).

Regardless of how their networks are set up, most HMOs (and a minority of PPOs) use a *gatekeeper model,* in which a primary care provider must approve the use of a specialist. In our 1994 national survey of HMOs and PPOs, we found that primary care providers were generally held responsible for referrals to most specialists in 92 percent of network/IPAs and 96 percent of group or staff HMOs (Gold and others, 1995a). In network/IPA models, these responsibilities were assigned typically to individual physicians, with 92 percent of plans requiring patients to choose a primary care physician. In contrast, only 61 percent of group or staff HMOs required patients to choose a primary care physician. In 1990, three-quarters of HMOs required primary care referrals for mental health services (Christianson, Wholey, and Peterson, 1997). A more recent study involving site visits to twenty-three HMOs across the nation showed comparable results, with about one-fifth of plans allowing self-referral for mental health or substance abuse services (Felt-Lisk, 1996). The option to self-refer is likely to increase, pushed by the recognition that choice is important to consumers.

Solid current information on provider arrangements in managed care plans for behavioral health services does not exist. In 1989, 44 percent of HMOs in a national survey said they contracted with an entity not part of the

HMO (Peterson, Christianson, and Wholey, 1992) for the delivery of mental health services. This included 38 percent of group or staff HMOs and 48 percent of network/IPA HMOs (Wholey, Christianson, and Peterson, 1996). HMOs having such contracts were more likely to use risk-based contracts (Christianson, Wholey, and Peterson, 1997). HMOs varied in their strategies for managing mental health care. Some used strategies focused on exclusion and careful screening of physicians, and required prior approval for referrals. Others used financial incentives rather than authorization requirements.

Reports in the trade press illustrate the diversity of arrangements across firms today ("HMO Strategies for . . . Benefits," 1997). A number of large insurance-based or publicly traded firms offer behavioral health care through corporate subsidiaries. Examples include Aetna/US HealthCare, Cigna HealthCare, Pacific Health Systems, Principal HealthSystems, United HealthCare Corporate, and WellPoint Health Networks. Other large companies such as Oxford Health Plans, Health Insurance Plan (HIP), and Harvard Pilgrim Health Plan handle such care "in house," although exactly what that means is unclear. At Oxford, for example, *in house* means contracting with independent vendors who supply such services. HIP and Harvard-Pilgrim, however, tend to provide such services through internal departments and some contracts with external providers. Whether such differences in arrangements reflect the general complexity and variation in provider network structure across health plans or discrete and independent decision making for behavioral health services is not clear.

Provider Payment Methods. Provider payment arrangements in HMOs differ from those in PPOs. About 90 percent of PPOs in 1994 used pure fee-for-service payment arrangements (with no other bonus or withhold) for primary care physicians; only about 10 percent of HMOs did (Gold and others, 1995a, 1995b). In group or staff model HMOs, payment typically involved capitating individual primary care physicians or paying them a salary. There are sometimes other financial incentives in the form of bonuses or withholds distributed on the basis of utilization, cost, productivity, quality and satisfaction, or other measures. In network/IPA model HMOs, capitation for primary care physicians was most common (used in 56 percent of plans), but fee-for-service was also common, with bonuses or withholds (28 percent) distributed on a basis similar to that in group or staff HMOs.

Risk sharing with specialists is less common than with primary care physicians in HMOs. Such arrangements appear to be growing and becoming more complex. Over half the HMOs in our 1994 national survey shared some risk with individual specialty physicians associated with the plan (Gold and others, 1995b). While 97 percent of PPOs paid their specialists on a pure fee-for-service basis, only 42 percent of network/IPA HMOs and 24 percent of group or staff HMOs did so. In network/IPAs, risk payments to specialists most typically involved fee-for-service with a bonus or withhold (34 percent), though 20 percent used capitation. In group or staff HMOs, 31 percent used capitation to pay specialists, 28 percent used bonuses or withholds with either salary or fee-for-service, and 17 percent used salary.

Another recent trend in payment for specialists within HMOs is the use of risk-based payments for groups of specialists. In our 1994 national survey, 69 percent of group or staff HMOs, 47 percent of network/IPA HMOs, but only 7 percent of PPOs said they capitated individual specialists (Gold and others, 1995a). Over three-quarters of the HMOs said such capitation was increasing. In network/IPAs using capitation, it was also the common form of payment for mental health providers (used by 42 percent of such plans but only by 9 percent of group or staff plans).

Features of Care Management. Logic suggests that it is easier to modify a contract than it is to change how care is delivered, how providers relate to one another, and how both physicians and patients think. Clinical integration thus lags behind the contractual changes that characterize managed care. Nonetheless, the early development of a managed care infrastructure has modified how we think about systems of care even if we are uncertain about the extent to which these conceptual changes have been translated into both actual physician practice patterns and the physician-patient relationship.

In our 1994 survey, virtually all the HMOs and from 72 to 79 percent of the PPOs said they have a written quality assurance plan, a quality assurance committee, and patient grievance procedures (Gold and others, 1995a). Over 90 percent of HMOs (and 59 percent of PPOs) said they have targeted quality improvement initiatives. All but 3 percent to 6 percent of HMOs do consumer surveys, as do 55 percent of PPOs. Virtually all the HMOs (and 45 percent of PPOs) said they conduct clinically focused studies on a regular basis. Formal written practice guidelines are used by 75 percent of each HMO group (but only 27 percent of PPOs), albeit typically in a few areas. Over three-quarters of the HMOs (and 52 percent of PPOs) said they profile practice patterns—most commonly to identify areas for systemwide improvement, for provider feedback, to screen outliers for review, and to make decisions on contract renewals.

The development of internal quality improvement systems has been encouraged by purchasers, with large purchasers commonly requiring plans to have accreditation from the National Committee on Quality Assurance (NCQA). In 1994, just under two-fifths of the HMOs in our survey were already NCQA accredited, and most of the rest were moving in that direction. HEDIS is an effort started by commercial purchasers (now joined by Medicare and Medicaid) working with health plans and others to develop performance standards for managed care (Grimaldi, 1997). Almost all the HMOs (59 percent of PPOs) in 1994 had reviewed the HEDIS specifications, with most either already generating indicators or planning to do so that year.

Implications for Managed Behavioral Health Care

More than 100 million of the 185.7 million people with private health insurance in 1994 were in plans with some type of program for managed behavioral health care (Iglehart, 1996). Even though utilization review and case management for a payer, along with employee assistance programs, are the most common roles for managed behavioral health care companies, risk-based contracting is the most rapidly growing activity for such firms, accounting for half their revenue (Frank, McGuire, and Newhouse, 1995). In private health plans, key features of such arrangements include care management and financing organized as a "specialty carve out," shared risk (called "soft" capitation), and competition for contracts rather than enrollees. Managed behavioral health care firms compete to be the sole contractor of managed behavioral health care services for a purchaser. This differs from the most common form of competition for general managed care, in which purchasers may choose several health plans for the same function, with each then competing for enrollees.

It is important to identify who is making the carve-out for behavioral health services and which individuals are affected. Carve-outs that involve benefits under which all employees are covered are not the same as carve-outs that depend on an employee's choice among conventional and managed care products offered by an employer. This distinction is particularly relevant when financial risk is a feature of the managed care plan, the carve-out plan, or both. In concept, the employer who carves out mental health benefits to an organization separate from the one that holds the general health contract assumes, one could argue, the responsibility for coordination across the two contracts. In contrast, when the managed care plan itself does the carve-out, it is the plan rather than the employer that is ultimately responsible for how well the two systems work together. This issue of responsibility becomes particularly relevant as behavioral health and general health needs overlap, giving rise to complementary services and making possible a considerable amount of interplay or substitution between treatments. For example, coordinating behavioral health and other health care could be more difficult if the latter is carved out by an employer and offered independently to employees who receive other health services, including pharmaceuticals, in separate managed care organizations that may be at risk for the costs of that care.

How best to conceptualize a behavioral health carve-out within a managed care plan is unclear. From one perspective, carve-outs are specific to behavioral health care coverage. They involve a recognition by the managed care plan that features unique to behavioral health care require specialized organizations and systems of care. From another perspective, however, these carve-outs could be viewed as one more example of the complexity involved in building a provider network within a managed care plan. Contracting for behavioral health involves decision processes that may be similar to those involved in contracting for cardiology or radiology services, or in selecting a specialty group. But behavioral health care organizations may be more complex and more highly structured than other systems of care (Kihlstrom, 1997). Whatever the case, it is essential to be clear on whether the purchaser or health plan is responsible for coordinating behavioral health services and to understand the increasingly complex arrangements between plans and providers.

References

American Association of Health Plans. *HMO and PPO Industry Profile (1995–1996 Edition)*. Washington D.C.: American Association of Health Plans, 1996.

Buck, J. A., and Umland, B. "Trends: Covering Mental Health and Substance Abuse Services." *Health Affairs*, 1997, *16*, 120–127.

Christianson, J. B., Wholey, D. R., and Peterson, M. S. "Strategies for Managing Services Delivery in HMOs: An Application to Mental Health Care." *Medical Care Research and Review*, 1997, *54*, 200–222.

Claxton, G., Feder, J., Shactman, D., and Altman, S. "Policy Issues in Nonprofit Conversions." *Health Affairs*, 1997, *16*, 9–28.

Corrigan, J., Eden, J., Gold, M., and Pickreign, J. "Trends Toward a National Health Care Marketplace." *Inquiry*, 1997, *34*, 11–28.

Felt-Lisk, S. "How HMOs Structure Primary Care." *Managed Care Quarterly*, 1996, *4*, 96–105.

Frank, R. G., Koyanagi, C., and McGuire, T. G. "The Politics and Economics of Mental Health 'Parity' Laws." *Health Affairs*, 1997, *16*, 108–119.

Frank, R. G., McGuire, T. G., and Newhouse, J. P. "Risk Contracts in Managed Mental Health Care." *Health Affairs*, 1995, *14*, 50–64.

Gold, M. R., and Hurley, R. "The Role of Managed Care 'Products' in Managed 'Care Plans.'" *Inquiry*, 1997, *34*, 29–37.

Gold, M. R., Hurley, R., Lake, T., Ensor, T., and Berenson, R. *Arrangements Between Managed Care Plans and Physicians: Results from a 1994 Survey of Managed Care Plans*. Selected External Research Series Number 3. Washington, D.C.: Physician Payment Review Commission, 1995a.

Gold, M. R., Hurley, R., Lake, T., Ensor, T., and Berenson, R. "A National Survey of the Arrangements Managed-Care Plans Make with Physicians." *New England Journal of Medicine*, 1995b, *333*, 1678–1683.

Gray, B. H. "Conversion of HMOs and Hospitals: What's at Stake?" *Health Affairs*, 1997, *16*, 29–47.

Grimaldi, P. L. "New HEDIS Means More Information about HMOs." *Journal of Health Care Finance*, 1997, *23*, 40–50.

Health Care Financing Administration. "Fact Sheet: Managed Care on Medicare and Medicaid." Washington, D.C.: Health Care Financing Administration, Jan. 1997.

"HMO Strategies for Managing Behavioral Health Benefits." *Managed Care Week*, July 21, 1997, pp. 6–7.

Iglehart, J. K. "Health Policy Report: Managed Care and Mental Health." *New England Journal of Medicine*, 1996, *334*, 131–135.

InterStudy. *The InterStudy Competitive Edge: Part II HMO Industry Report*, No. 7.2. Excelsior, Minn.: InterStudy, Oct. 1997.

Jensen, G., Morrisey, M., Gaffney, S., and Liston, D. K. "The New Dominance of Managed Care: Insurance Trends in the 1990s." *Health Affairs*, 1997, *16*, 125–136.

Kihlstrom, L. C. "Trends: Characteristics and Growth of Managed Behavioral Health Firms." *Health Affairs*, 1997, *16*, 127–130.

Peterson, M. S., Christianson, J. B., and Wholey, D. R. *National Survey of Mental Health, Alcohol, and Drug Abuse Treatment in HMOs: 1989 Chartbook*. Excelsior, Minn.: InterStudy, 1992.

Shadle, M., and Christianson, J. B. "The Impact of HMO Development on Mental Health and Chemical Dependency Services." *Hospital and Community Psychiatry*, 1989, *40*, 1145–1151.

Shortell, S. M., and Hull, K. E. "The New Organization of the Health Care Delivery System." In S. H. Altman and U. Reinhardt (eds.), *Strategic Choices for a Changing Health Care System*. Ann Arbor, Mich.: Health Administration Press, 1996.

Wholey, D. R., Christianson, J. B., and Peterson, M. "Organization of Mental Health Care in HMOs." *Administration and Policy in Mental Health*, 1996, *23*, 307–328.

MARSHA GOLD is a senior fellow, Mathematica Policy Research, Washington, D.C.

This chapter examines ethical issues encountered in the allocation of limited behavioral health care resources.

Behavioral Health: A View from the Industry

Richard C. Surles, Robert J. Fox

The term *managed behavioral care* encompasses a variety of programs and technological applications. A useful conceptual framework for managed behavioral care divides the industry's product array into five segments: (1) administrative services only (ASO), which is not risk based; (2) utilization review; (3) employee assistance program (EAP); (4) integrated management; and (5) full risk. As indicated in Figure 3.1, the role of a managed behavioral care organization (MBCO) differs markedly across the product array. Product segments vary in their intensity of care management, levels of risk, and amount of revenue, ranging from the purely administrative service and provider network model at one extreme to the full-risk, capitated product at the other. Each product type imbues "managed behavioral care" with a different meaning, with risk-based capitated products representing the most volatile mix of potentially positive and negative implications.

The expansion of risk-based managed behavioral care capitation programs, which grew from 13.6 million enrollees in 1993 to 32 million enrollees (22 percent of industry enrollment) in 1997, is an important industry trend (Oss, Drissel, and Clary, 1997, p. 22). Although risk arrangements are becoming more common, capitation payment rates have remained, at best, stagnant in recent years. The broader use of risk-based capitated programs has contributed to increased scrutiny of MBCO practices.

The business success of managed behavioral care has been testimony to the eagerness of payers and managed care organizations (MCOs) to embrace the industry's basic methods. Yet managed behavioral care technology has elicited passionate objections, especially from professional societies and consumer advocacy groups. Though arguments against the industry have been

Figure 3.1 Managed Behavioral Care: A Range of Meaning

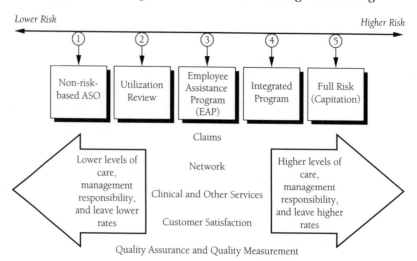

many-faceted, the central accusation continues to be that managed behavioral care generates cost savings by denying care. However, this message tends to foster a narrow debate that ignores the factors that led to the industry's development and neglects to identify ways of working to refine and improve mental health services.

With limited health care resources, difficult decisions are being made about who receives care and the amount and types of care provided. Due to the newness of managed care technology and its cost containment aspects, managed behavioral care has been a primary target in public policy debates about access to care. Unfortunately, issues that have been in existence much longer than the industry, such as discriminatory limitations on behavioral health benefits, are frequently cast as symptoms of managed behavioral care alone.

In general, debates about the challenges in behavioral care service delivery have been narrowly focused on perceived MBCO shortcomings. Yet the debate needs to address the full range of decision-making processes and participants in behavioral care purchasing and delivery. Participants must seek out ways of effectively allocating limited resources, as well as better means of achieving parity of mental health and substance abuse coverage, and better indicators of quality and outcomes.

The allocation of limited resources entails policy and administrative issues that extend well beyond the province of MBCOs (Surles, 1995). The often-conflicting objectives of major behavioral health participants (payers, health care plans and MCOs, MBCOs, enrollees, and providers) intermingle to create a range of financial, health care, and professional responsibility issues. Specifically, transactions involving the purchase of managed behavioral care services raise a number of potential ethical dilemmas. Each participant in the purchasing process makes choices that affect the nature and extent of behavioral care delivery. For example, in selecting a health benefits plan, a payer may weigh various factors, including premium levels, out-of-pocket costs to enrollees, and care access and quality. In a payer's negotiations with a health plan or MCO, both parties maneuver toward a mutually acceptable balance on benefit plan design aspects affecting cost, quality, and access. Fundamental choices and ethical determinations are made that greatly influence the allocation of health care resources. Numerous questions may be answered either explicitly or implicitly: Will behavioral health care benefits be purchased from the health plan or MCO or directly from an MBCO? Will the payer and health plan or MCO share the financial risk? Will nondiscriminatory behavioral benefits in parity with other health benefits be offered? How much money is the payer willing to spend on premiums or administrative fees? What clinical and administrative measurements will be used to assess the health plan's performance? In the process of designing the benefit plan, the payer and the health plan or MCO decide upon an acceptable—but imperfect—combination of solutions to ethical questions about cost, quality, and access.

Social and Ethical Questions

If the health plan or MCO contracts on a subcapitation basis with an MBCO or with provider groups for the behavioral care program, other issues become evident: Should the payer's preferred behavioral care benefit design be employed, or might careful management of an unlimited behavioral benefit be more effective? What performance measures will be applied to the MBCO or provider groups and at what subcontract price? If the payer has budgeted an amount of funds for behavioral care, will those funds be allocated appropriately to the MBCO or the provider groups through subcapitation? For example, in a typical Medicaid plan managed by an HMO, the HMO is paid a capitated rate by the state for all general medical and behavioral health services. The HMO assumes the financial risk for providing the necessary care. Some HMOs, in turn, subcontract or subcapitate to MBCOs or provider groups for mental health and substance abuse treatment services. However, though most MBCOs have the requisite levels of experience and sophistication in pricing for such services, not all subcapitated entities have the skills needed to responsibly manage the financial risk. In one infamous case, a state reportedly paid an HMO more than $30 per enrolled member per month intended for behavioral care. The HMO, in turn, subcapitated to an MBCO for a subcapitation rate of only $6 per member per month. The MBCO failed financially and, due to service shortfalls, providers and enrollees developed an intense animosity toward managed care. However, during this period the HMO made record profits that were mainly attributable to the disparate capitation and subcapitation amounts allocated for behavioral care. The ultimate harm was the failure to deliver appropriate, accessible care to those in need.

Though managed behavioral care has been the most visible target for criticism in such cases, the financial and ethical issues require a broader sharing of accountability. Many MCOs set subcapitation on commercial behavioral care contracts at rates between $2 and $3 per member per month or about 3 percent of total premium (Petrila, 1996, p. 373). These rates stand in stark contrast to the estimated 8 percent to 10 percent of total health care expenditures accounted for by behavioral care.

The previous example of the Medicaid HMO program suggests that, without proper safeguards, the competing interests of multiple participants can yield poor results. The basic resource allocation decisions affecting the well-being of enrollees in managed behavioral health programs are not made by MBCOs alone, and the best solutions can be devised only with broad participation.

Additional ethical tensions occur within interactions involving MBCOs, providers, and patients and consumers. Providers have a fiduciary duty to serve the best interests of their patients. However, capitated providers must balance the service needs of the individual patient with the resource interests of all their patients. Moreover, providers must pursue their own economic interests. Given limited resources, imperfect reconciliations of individual patient, patient population, and provider interests result.

These imperfect results have also been characteristic of fee-for-service systems. Provider "gaming" of fee-for-service reimbursement procedure coding systems has not always been conducted merely in the patient's economic interest, but also has been a way of increasing provider income (Gray, 1997). Gaming is a rejection of resource limitations established by payers and health plans and is a primary force behind the growth of managed care. Under fee-for-service, payer and health plan discord with providers is essentially tacit and covert. Managed care exposes this disharmony of interests—it does not create it.

Managed care has the potential to either exacerbate or relieve ethical tensions. Particularly within capitated managed behavioral care programs, providers can have greater flexibility to spend behavioral health dollars based on their professional assessments of individual patient and patient population needs. Although the defined funding levels and risk sharing of capitation promote cost-efficiency, there also can be an incentive to underserve consumers. Undertreatment in a managed behavioral care system and overutilization in a fee-for-service system usually spring from the same systemic flaw: a lack of agreement on care delivery practice standards within the context of established funding allocations. As the use of capitation expands, so does the need for broad-based, cooperative resolution of practice and allocation issues.

Conclusion

Focusing on the perceived perils of managed behavioral care can be a means of avoiding more crucial issues. Many of the most vehement criticisms of MBCOs are rooted, in effect, in a demand that managed care somehow unilaterally resolve major public policy issues. But public acknowledgment of the growing need to "balance the possibilities of medicine and public expectations against the willingness to finance them" is not yet widespread (Mechanic, 1997, p. 83).

Progress in behavioral care practice and resource allocations must be built upon informed cooperation. A clearer mutual recognition and acceptance of the roles and responsibilities of all participants in managed behavioral care would be a good first step. Accelerating trends of payer and consumer involvement in performance measurement processes are a positive sign. With enhanced input from consumers, providers, MCOs, payers, MBCOs, government agencies, and academic institutions, better assessments of quality and outcomes can be achieved. Armed with more objective measures of care efficacy, difficult resource allocation issues may be easier to resolve. When we have better evidence about what works, we will have a more rational basis for properly allocating limited resources.

During the past decade, the specialty managed behavioral care industry has grown to cover over 66 percent of the insured population in the United States (Oss, Drissel, and Clary, 1997, p. 5). The industry has matured rapidly from simple precertification techniques to sophisticated systems of preferred provider networks and risk management of complex patient problems. And the new technology has become a favored tool for controlling costs while making more appropriate use of a wider variety of treatment and service settings. However, some slowing of growth and significant market consolidation began to occur by late 1996. Ultimately, the future of the industry will depend less on rapid business expansion and more on the ability to consistently and effectively manage the delivery of high-quality care and positive outcomes. Realizing the full potential of this future will require the constructive cooperation of all participants in managed behavioral care.

References

Gray, B. H. "Trust and Trustworthy Care in the Managed Care Era." *Health Affairs,* 1997, *16,* 34–49.

Mechanic, D. "Muddling Through Elegantly: Finding the Proper Balance in Rationing." *Health Affairs,* 1997, *16,* 83–92.

Oss, M. E., Drissel, A. B., and Clary, J. *Managed Behavioral Health Market Share in the United States, 1997–1998.* Gettysburg, Pa.: OPEN MINDS, 1997.

Petrila, J. "Ethics, Money, and the Problem of Coercion in Managed Behavioral Health Care." *St. Louis University Law Journal,* 1996, *40,* 359–405.

Surles, R. C. "Perspectives: Broadening the Ethical Analysis of Managed Care." *Health Affairs,* 1995, *14,* 29–31.

RICHARD C. SURLES is president of clinical systems at Merit Behavioral Care Corporation, Park Ridge, New Jersey. He was formerly commissioner of the New York State Office of Mental Health.

ROBERT J. FOX is director of planning at Merit Behavioral Care Corporation, Park Ridge, New Jersey.

Increasing external review of mental health services raises serious concerns about needed patient advocacy.

Utilization Review and the Treatment of Mental Illness: Emerging Norms and Variabilities

Mark Schlesinger

The various forms of managed care that have become a common feature in American medicine have the potential to dramatically alter the treatment of mental illness and substance abuse (often called *behavioral health care)* (Pincus, Zarin, and West, 1996). But this variety has also confused the discussion of mental health policy, which often refers to managed care in some loosely defined generic manner (Schlesinger, 1995). The one clear lesson that has emerged from the past twenty-five years of research on HMOs, PPOs, and the other acronymic entities that make up the managed care industry is that the term *managed care* encompasses a wide variety of practices and policies and that only by focusing on particular features of managed care can one sensibly anticipate its consequences for different illnesses. More specifically, research has demonstrated that outcomes in terms of costs and quality of care depend on these factors: the specific means the plan uses in its attempts to influence clinical practice (for example, financial incentives versus administrative constraints); broad characteristics of the plan itself (its legal ownership, whether it is locally controlled or affiliated with a national corporation, its degree of centralization of provider networks); and the conditions under which the plan operates (for example, the extent of market competition it faces and the local norms of treatment in its area).

Here I narrow the focus of analysis to the practice of utilization review (UR), found in virtually every sort of managed care plan. Indeed, UR is in many ways the common denominator among disparate forms of managed care. Research suggests that external review can substantially alter the costs and clinical practices associated with the treatment of mental illness (Mechanic, Schlesinger, and McAlpine, 1995; Hodgkin, 1992). Apart from the implications for patient care, the application of external review raises important questions about professional authority and autonomy (Sabin and Daniels, 1994; Tischler, 1990).

Although there is a modest literature linking the existence of a UR program to measures of cost or utilization for behavioral health care, none of these studies offer much insight into *how* external review affects clinical practices. Summaries of past studies of utilization review (Schlesinger, Gray, and Perreira, 1997) suggest that UR could have three broad types of influence on clinicians: constraining their autonomy to treat patients in ways they deem appropriate, increasing the costs of advocating for their patients' interests (by making the appeals process within UR time-consuming or frustrating), or reducing their perceived authority by requiring extensive documentation of clinical claims or allowing reviewers to deny treatment even if the reviewer lacks comparable professional training to that of the clinician. Although none of these influences are necessarily problematic—constraints may be quite appropriate if the original clinical practices were ill-conceived or unnecessary—they may all be experienced by clinicians as undesirable events. And each *could* have negative consequences for patient care, even the seemingly trivial hassles in the third category, if loss of authority undermines the willingness of clinicians to advocate for care they believe to be effective (Lee and Etheridge, 1989). Equally important, because the treatment of mental illness differs in certain important ways from the treatment of other medical conditions, review practices that may on balance improve the quality of care for most conditions may be more problematic when applied to mental health care (Mechanic, Schlesinger, and McAlpine, 1995).

Research also demonstrates that styles of UR vary tremendously, both for medical care generally (Schlesinger, Gray, and Perreira, 1997) and for mental health care in particular (Garnick and others, 1994). When the practice was first applied to psychiatric services in the mid-1980s, the review process was often contracted to an outside agency, which we will refer to as a utilization review organization (URO) (Englund, 1994). Although most UROs reviewed the treatment of mental illness along with a variety of other medical or surgical treatments (in a type of review referred to here as *inclusive plans*), some concentrated on behavioral health care. By the 1990s, these specialized plans developed their own networks of affiliated providers and the capacity to more actively manage services (Englund, 1994). As they evolved, these plans came to resemble a sort of specialized HMO, and the term *carve-out* was coined to describe them. By 1994, the treatment of more than a hundred million Americans was overseen by companies specializing in managed behavioral care, with UROs still the most common (thirty-seven million covered lives) and carve-out plans the fastest growing (over twenty million covered lives) (Frank, McGuire, and Newhouse, 1995).

In this context, it becomes important to explore whether utilization review functions differently or has different consequences in specialized plans compared to inclusive plans. Because specialized plans may develop greater expertise in treating mental illness, they may become more aggressive in transforming clinical practices (Wolff and Schlesinger, 1998). Inclusive plans, however, may inadvertently disrupt clinical norms because they are less aware of the ways in which mental illness differs from other medical conditions. Thus specialization is likely to play an important mediating factor in the application of UR to mental health care.

There is little in the published literature that addresses this comparison. But by drawing data from some recently completed (and as yet unpublished) studies and reanalyzing them, we can get some additional insights. The first data come from a national survey conducted in 1993, which collected data from 102 UROS, 13 specializing in behavioral health care (Wolff and Schlesinger, 1998; Schlesinger, Dorwart, and Epstein, 1996). These data will help us explore how the process of external review differs between mental health and other medical conditions. Our second source of data is a survey conducted in 1996 of 1,647 psychologists practicing in the state of New Jersey (Rothbaum and others, forthcoming), reporting provider experiences with ten different managed care plans; half carve-out plans, half inclusive HMOs.

Background: Literature Review

Early evaluations of UR programs under private insurance suggested that external review could significantly reduce the costs of mental health care, but provided little information about quality of care or outcomes for patients (Hodgkin, 1992). Subsequent studies found similar patterns of cost saving for public sector programs such as Medicaid, with little negative response by clinicians (Callahan and others, 1994). But other reviews noted that the evidence of substantial cost savings in both public and private sectors had come from employer groups that had previously had above-average costs for behavioral health care (Mechanic, Schlesinger, and McAlpine, 1995). These are exactly the purchasers likely to be first to adopt external review.

Utilization review alters treatment by comparing prevailing clinical practices to some standards or criteria. For high-cost populations, review firms can simply invoke prevailing practices for the population as a whole as the relevant standard. This may constrain costs without being seen as unduly intrusive into clinical autonomy. However, to produce comparable savings for a broader population, reviewers limit utilization *below* prevailing norms for the profession. This is certain to generate stronger reactions from clinicians and potentially more problematic outcomes for patients.

The very limited literature that compares review practices between mental illness and other medical conditions provides some indirect support for the growing impact of external review for psychiatric treatment. Early surveys suggested that UR became an important influence in the treatment of mental health care later than for many other conditions. As of 1988, for example, only 18 percent of psychiatrists reported that they "frequently or always" needed to obtain approval prior to hospitalizing a patient; 36 percent indicated that they never had to do so (Schlesinger, Dorwart, and Epstein, 1996). But external review was more extensive once a patient was admitted to the hospital; 27 percent of the psychiatrists reported that they were "frequently or always" being pressured by insurance companies to discharge their patients earlier than they would have preferred.

A subsequent survey conducted by the American Medical Association in 1990 suggested that UR was rapidly increasing in mental health care. Psychiatrists responding to the survey were more likely than other physicians to report that external review was "interfering with clinical decision making" (26 percent versus 21 percent for all physicians) (Emmons and Chawla, 1991). They also reported spending more time dealing with external reviewers (3.2 hours per week compared to an average of 2.1 hours per week) and more frequently reported having requested admissions denied by external review. As in the earlier survey, the primary impact of external review on mental health care appeared to involve concurrent review of hospitalizations. Almost 60 percent of psychiatrists reported that concurrent review was the most intrusive and time-consuming form of UR (compared to only 20 percent for other physicians).

The published literature provides only fragmentary evidence on the impact of external review on the clinical practices of mental health professionals. Data from a national survey of UROs operating in 1993 reveals that external review of mental health care demands more extensive information from clinicians (particularly about treatment plan) than that required for review of other medical conditions, but is somewhat less likely to apply standardized protocols to psychiatric hospitalizations than to other medical conditions (Wolff and Schlesinger, 1998). This study also revealed significant variations in practice among UROs. For example, while the majority of review firms left the determination of appropriateness of hospitalization for adolescent depression (our "tracer condition") to the discretion of individual reviewers, about 11 percent relied heavily on standardized protocols. Although most UROs took into account the adamancy of the treating clinician when making these decisions about hospitalization, 14 percent reported that they never allowed this to influence their decisions about admissions.

A study of psychologists by Rothbaum and colleagues (forthcoming) further documents the focus of mental health UR on length of stay in the hospital: only 3.4 percent of respondents reported that they had difficulty getting necessary hospital admissions for their patients due to external review, but 20.5 percent reported that they had been "forced to discharge before patient is clinically ready." This survey also provided further documentation for the prevalence of the hassle factor. Forty-three percent of respondents reported being burdened by the paperwork of external review, while 30 percent complained that they were forced to deal with "untrained" or "less well-trained" reviewers. The New Jersey survey also provided information on the more recent spread of external review to outpatient care; a third of all respondents felt that their primary managed care plan had not authorized a sufficient number of sessions for their patients. Again, this study found tremendous variation among review practices. For example, 63 percent of respondents affiliated with the most intrusive plan expressed complaints about paperwork, but less than 25 percent of the psychologists affiliated with the least intrusive plan expressed similar complaints.

Measures of the Review Process. I suggested earlier that the impact of external review can be sensibly disaggregated into three broad forms of influence: the intrusiveness of review protocols in term of limiting clinical autonomy, the openness of the appeals process to make exceptions in response to the circumstances of individual patients, and the hassle factor for clinicians facing extensive paperwork or reviewers who in clinicians' assessment lack appropriate training.

Research has demonstrated that some approaches to external review offer a great deal of latitude for the treating clinician, while others force treatment practices to conform to a strictly defined set of standards (Schlesinger, Gray, and Perreira, 1997). Although it is unclear which of these approaches leads to better care or a more appropriate balancing of the costs and quality of treatment, it is apparent that under any approach to review, there will often be errors made in the initial stages of the process. No standardized protocol or individual reviewer's judgment is good enough to escape a substantial error rate, probably on the order of 20 to 30 percent, compared to expert judgments of appropriate treatment (Rubin and others, 1992).

Consequently, the willingness and ability of clinicians to appeal initial denials when they see them as inappropriate is a crucial part of the UR process. But here too, research suggests that managed care firms vary greatly in terms of the openness and responsiveness of their appeals process (Schlesinger, Gray, and Perreira, 1997). Indeed, some firms increase the intensity of external review for clinicians who show themselves to be consistently at variance with review protocols. Under these circumstances, clinicians are indirectly penalized when they appeal a case, because high rates of appeal are likely to increase their expected costs from UR in the future. Extensive hassles may discourage clinicians from seeking authorization for treatment at all. In addition, they may discourage clinicians from appealing cases in which the initial review led to an erroneous decision.

Constraints on Clinical Autonomy. The national URO survey found that as of 1993, the average initial denial rate for requested hospitalization for adolescent depression was 11 percent. (This relatively low percentage, however, is somewhat deceptive. If one counts requests where the URO negotiated with the clinician to instead treat solely on an outpatient basis—termed *conversions* in the industry—and requests where the clinician never fully pursued the request to a final decision—termed *withdrawals*—then 26 percent of all initial requests did not result in hospitalization.) The average target length-of-stay (LOS) for adolescents who were hospitalized for depression was just under ten days. About one-fifth of all UROs had initial denial rates in excess of 20 percent;

another fifth had denial rates of under 5 percent. About a quarter of all UROs had a target LOS of less than a week. Twelve percent had targets of greater than two weeks.

While relatively few psychologists reported having problems obtaining hospitalization for their patients when it was needed, many more felt that the managed care firms authorized an inadequate number of outpatient visits. But the prevalence of problems with admissions was twice as high for some firms as for the average in the state of New Jersey; there was considerably less variation in reported problems with obtaining a sufficient number of outpatient visits.

Average denial rates for requested admissions for mental illness are reported on the URO survey to be 20 percent to 25 percent higher than for other forms of medical treatment, though this difference is not statistically significant. Neither the URO survey nor the New Jersey survey of psychologists revealed any significant differences in constraints on admission practices to hospitals between specialized and inclusive forms of managed care. But the psychologists reported a significantly higher frequency of problems obtaining a sufficient number of outpatient visits from the specialized firms (38 percent) than from the inclusive firms (27 percent).

Other differences emerge from measures of review flexibility. For the most part, review of hospitalizations for adolescent depression does not appear to be particularly standardized in either absolute terms or by comparison to other medical conditions. Seventy-five percent of UROs report relying primarily on reviewer discretion in determining the acceptability of an admission for adolescent depression (compared to 48 percent for other medical conditions). On average, 30 percent of these admissions are reported to exceed the target LOS (compared to an average of less than 20 percent for other medical conditions). Eighty percent of psychologists in New Jersey reported no problems with being forced to prematurely discharge patients from the hospital, and only 12 percent report pressure to rely on medication as the primary method of treating mental illness.

Here again, there is considerable variation in industry practices, with clear evidence that in some managed care settings external review is quite inflexible and unresponsive to clinicians. Eleven percent of UROs rely primarily on formal criteria for evaluating admissions for adolescent depression. Twenty-seven percent of review firms allow no more than 10 percent of their admissions to exceed the target length of stay; 9 percent reported that less than 2 percent of their admissions exceeded the targets. Fourteen percent of the firms indicated that they "never" take the adamancy of the treating clinician into account in authorizing admissions for adolescent depression. Restrictive practices of one form or another are found in about 25 percent to 30 percent of the industry. Although there was less variation in measures of review flexibility in the psychologist survey, respondents did suggest that one managed care firm was much less flexible than the average: 30 percent of clinicians affiliated with this company reported being pressured to prematurely discharge patients and 19 percent to rely on medication as the primary treatment modality.

This less flexible plan was one of the mental health carve-out plans operating in New Jersey. Specialized plans as a group were reported by psychologists to be less flexible, particularly in terms of favoring medication (15 versus 8 percent). Among UROs, specialized plans were significantly more likely to adopt structured criteria for determining whether a requested admission for depression was appropriate.

Accessibility of the UR Appeals Process. Given the challenges of defining appropriate care for mental illness, one might expect that the appeals process would be particularly important. But the proportion of initial denials that are successfully appealed in specialty UROs averaged only 7 percent. This contrasts with a successful appeal rate of almost 20 percent for all the conditions reviewed by inclusive UROs. Forty-one percent of the firms specializing in the review of mental health care had successful appeal rates of 2 percent or less.

Low rates of successful appeal may reflect either different practices on the part of specialized review firms or a reduced willingness or ability on the part of mental health care professionals to advocate for their patients. Unfortunately, we have no direct measures of providers' willingness to vigorously pursue an appeal. We do, however, have some sense of review practices that might influence appeals. UROs report that they are somewhat *more* responsive to the adamancy of the clinician in making decisions about admissions for psychiatric illness than for other illnesses. And the costs associated with appeals appear to be lower in review organizations that specialize in mental health care. They have significantly lower telephone abandonment rates (2 percent versus 5 percent) and significantly shorter elapsed time between requests and decisions about authorizing hospitalizations (0.5 days versus 0.91 days). Specialty UROs are also much less likely (50 percent versus 87 percent) to intensify their review process for clinicians whose practices consistently conflict with review criteria.

Taken together, these data suggest that lower rates of successful appeal for psychiatric care are not the result of administrative obstacles to appeals. The data from the psychologists, however, conflict with the national findings on UROs. Psychologists affiliated with carve-out plans are significantly more likely (28.0 versus 10.8 percent) to report lengthy delays during precertification for hospital admissions. If the URO data are accurate, they suggest that low rates of successful appeal are a consequence either of less effective advocacy by clinicians or an appeal process that works less successfully for inpatient mental health care.

The Hassle Factor. Both surveys suggest that hassles are an important source of dissatisfaction for mental health care professionals. This is most evident with respect to paperwork demands, which represent the single most common problem reported on the survey of New Jersey psychologists. The URO survey verifies that providers treating mental illness are more likely than those treating other medical conditions to be asked to file information on their treatment plans, but are not expected to convey more about diagnostic tests or medical history. Managed care plans that specialize in mental health care appear to be most demanding of information. They are more likely than inclusive managed care plans to request information on both medical history (85 percent versus 63 percent) and diagnostic tests (46 percent versus 27 percent). The carve-out plans in New Jersey were more frequently seen as producing excessive paperwork (57 percent of their affiliated providers compared to 32 percent of providers in other plans).

Because information on the professional training of reviewers was not collected for particular diagnoses, we can only compare the practices of specialty and inclusive UROs. UROs that specialized in mental health care reported that they *never* used either clerical staff or LPNs to review cases or even to collect preliminary information. In comparison, 12 percent of the inclusive firms used less well-trained reviewers, though only a handful allowed them to issue denials of admission. The results from the New Jersey survey, however, were not entirely consistent with the national URO survey. Psychologists were more likely to complain of "untrained or less well-trained" reviewers when affiliated with carve-out plans (34 percent versus 25 percent).

Conclusion

On average, mental health care providers do not appear to confront significantly more problematic review practices than their colleagues treating other medical conditions. Indeed, in terms of both flexibility within the review process and the training of personnel used to make review decisions, UR for mental health care seems to largely avoid many of the practices that most trouble clinicians. But the relatively benign quality of modal practices can mask the intrusive and highly standardized character of a modest number of managed care firms reviewing mental health care. And the firms that specialize in mental health care—the fastest-growing part of the managed care industry—appear to be significantly more intrusive and problematic than inclusive managed care plans for clinicians.

It should be emphasized that the greater intrusiveness of the specialty UROs and carve-out firms need not be seen as a negative attribute of these plans. One might expect that these specialty firms would develop greater experience and expertise, making them more able and willing to challenge questionable clinical practices (Wolff and Schlesinger, 1998). Specialty plans may thus be better able to eliminate inappropriate and unnecessarily expensive treatment. Although the carve-out plans in New Jersey were significantly more likely to be seen as imposing excessive paperwork or long delays in precertifying hospital admissions, they were no more likely to be seen as denying a necessary admission than more inclusive HMOs.

There is no reason to presume, however, that specialty plans will necessarily use their greater ability to reshape clinical practice in ways that reflect the broader goals of society. If managed care plans apply the same standards of medical necessity to mental health care that are used for assessing the appropriateness of other forms of medical treatment, they are likely to authorize an inadequate level of treatment as viewed from the societal perspective (Sabin and Daniels, 1994). For example, conditions like substance abuse that impose large costs on family members or other residents of the community may merit treatment even if the intervention is not strictly medically necessary from the standpoint of the individual patient (Schlesinger, 1997). It is therefore noteworthy that the limited evidence that distinguishes the impact of UR on the treatment of substance abuse suggests that it reduces access to inpatient treatment without a corresponding increase in outpatient care (Mechanic, Schlesinger, and McAlpine, 1995).

Apart from concern with the externalities associated with certain mental illnesses, the most problematic aspect of the findings reported here involves the low rates of successful appeal in review organizations that specialize in mental health care. Fifty-eight percent of these UROs had successful appeal rates of 3 percent or less. It is almost certain that the error rate in initial reviews is at least several times higher than this (Rubin and others, 1992). Either too few legitimate cases are being appealed or the UR firms are being insufficiently responsive to providers' efforts at advocacy. Whichever is the case, a high rate of unsuccessful appeal creates its own natural feedback, further discouraging clinicians who would otherwise be inclined to contest an initial denial of care. If provider advocacy is curtailed, it imbalances the entire set of relationships that are necessary for external review to appropriately weigh the costs and quality of mental health care.

Concerns related either to externalities or to the appeals process could be addressed through state regulation of managed care. Although states have recently been quite active at addressing particular managed care practices, they have generally done little directly relevant to either of these concerns (Miller, 1997). (A minority of states—approximately ten at last count—have passed laws that try to protect providers' ability to advocate for their patients, which may indirectly help in terms of appeals.) Indeed, apart from some minimal requirements for due process, there is little external oversight over the entire UR appeals process. The stakes are too high for these omissions to continue. The spread of utilization review to mental health care has clearly had a substantial effect on clinical practices. It is essential that policymakers develop the institutional mechanisms to ensure that this influence adequately reflects the broader societal values relevant to mental illness and adequately protects the well-being of individuals in need of mental health care.

References

Callahan, J. J., Shepard, D. S., Beinecke, R. H., Larson, M. J., and Cavanaugh, D. *Evaluation of the Massachusetts Medicaid Mental Health/Substance Abuse Program.* Waltham, Mass.: Heller School for Advanced Studies in Social Welfare, 1994.

Emmons, D., and Chawla, A. "Physician Perceptions of the Intrusiveness of Utilization Review." In W. Margruder (ed.), *Socioeconomic Characteristics of Medical Practice.* Chicago: American Medical Association, 1991.

Englund, M. J. "From Fee-for-Service to Accountable Health Plans." In R. Schreter, S. Sharfstein, and C. Schreter (eds.), *Allies and Adversaries: The Impact of Managed Care on Mental Health Services.* Washington D.C.: American Psychiatric Press, 1994.

Frank, R. G., McGuire, T. G., and Newhouse, J. P. "Risk Contracts in Managed Mental Health Care." *Health Affairs,* 1995, *14,* 50–64.

Garnick, D. W., Hendricks, A. M., Dulski, J. D., Thorpe, K. E., and Horgan, C. "Characteristics of Private Sector Managed Care for Mental Health and Substance Abuse Treatment." *Hospital and Community Psychiatry,* 1994, *45,* 1201–1205.

Hodgkin, D. "The Impact of Private Utilization Management on Psychiatric Care: A Review of the Literature." *Journal of Mental Health Administration,* 1992, *19,* 143–157.

Lee, P., and Etheridge, L. "Clinical Freedom: Two Lessons for the U.K. from U.S. Experience with Privatization of Health Care." *Lancet,* 1989, *337,* 263–265.

Mechanic, D., Schlesinger, M., and McAlpine, D. "Management of Mental Health and Substance Abuse Services: State of the Art and Early Results." *Milbank Quarterly,* 1995, *73,* 19–55.

Miller, T. E. "Managed Care Regulation: In the Laboratory of the States." *Journal of the American Medical Association,* 1997, *278,* 1102–1109.

Pincus, H. A., Zarin, D. A., and West, J. C. "Peering into the 'Black Box': Measuring Outcomes of Managed Care." *Archives of General Psychiatry,* 1996, *53,* 870–877.

Rothbaum, P., Bernstein, D., Haller, O., Phelps, R., and Kohout, J. "New Jersey Psychologists Report on Managed Mental Health Care." *Professional Psychology: Research and Practice,* forthcoming.

Rubin, H. R., Rogers, W. H., Kahn, K., Rubenstein, L., and Brooks, R. "Watching the Doctor-Watchers: How Well Do Peer Review Organization Methods Detect Hospital Quality Problems?" *Journal of the American Medical Association,* 1992, *267,* 2349–2354.

Sabin, J., and Daniels, N. "Determining 'Medical Necessity' in Mental Health Practice." *Hastings Center Report,* 1994, *24,* 5–13.

Schlesinger, M. "Ethical Issues in Policy Advocacy." *Health Affairs,* 1995, *14,* 23–29.

Schlesinger, M. "Countervailing Agency: A Strategy of Principled Regulation Under Managed Competition." *Milbank Quarterly,* 1997, *75,* 35–87.

Schlesinger, M., Dorwart, R. A., and Epstein, S. "Managed Care Constraints on Psychiatrists' Hospital Practices: Bargaining Power and Professional Autonomy." *American Journal of Psychiatry,* 1996, *152,* 256–260.

Schlesinger, M. J., Gray, B. H., and Perreira, K. M. "Medical Professionalism Under Managed Care: The Pros and Cons of Utilization Review." *Health Affairs,* 1997, *16,* 106–124.

Tischler, G. L. "Utilization Management and the Quality of Care." *Hospital and Community Psychiatry,* 1990, *41,* 1099–1102.

Wolff, N., and Schlesinger, M. "Risk, Motives and Styles of Utilization Review: A Cross-Condition Comparison." *Social Science and Medicine,* 1998.

MARK SCHLESINGER *is associate professor of public health at Yale University and visiting associate research professor at the Institute for Health, Health Care Policy and Aging Research at Rutgers University.*

Behavioral health care carve-outs provide efficiencies of specialization; direct payer carve-outs also eliminate risk selection.

The Economics of Behavioral Health Carve-Outs

Richard G. Frank, Thomas G. McGuire

Health insurance plans have historically structured coverage for mental health and substance abuse care differently from coverage for other types of health care. In a finding that repeats the results from earlier work, the 1994–1995 surveys of employers' health benefits offerings conducted by the Bureau of Labor Statistics (1995) indicate that 93 percent of employer-based health plans restrict coverage for mental health benefits more than that for other illnesses. Mental health benefits are now often part of carve-out programs in public and private insurance plans charged with managing mental health costs. While the practice is not unique to mental health services, mental health is the area of care most frequently carved out. Carve-out programs manage mental health (and often substance abuse) in a different manner from other illnesses in the main plan, whether as part of an HMO or a managed indemnity contract. It is natural to wonder whether this discrimination in the treatment of mental health in terms of management represents a continuation of historical discrimination. In this chapter we address this issue by explaining what a carve-out is from an insurance perspective and what role a carve-out might play from the perspective of a payer. The ultimate effect of a carve-out is an empirical question we are learning more about, but understanding the conceptual role of a carve-out is an important first step in developing a broader understanding of its effect on access to and use of mental health services.

Carve-out arrangements involve separating segments of insurance risk—defined by service or disease—from the overall insurance risk and covering them in a separate contract. The contract is between the payer (employer, HMO) and the carve-out vendor. The employee as plan member is typically unaware of any such arrangement. These separate contracts delegate management of mental health services to specialized vendors. Carve-outs come in two general forms: one we will refer to as a *payer carve-out* (Frank, Huskamp, McGuire, and New-house, 1996), and the other we will label a *health plan subcontract*. In the first, an enrollee chooses a health plan for coverage of health care other than mental health, but must enroll with the carve-out vendor for mental health care. There are many examples of this type of arrangement, and variants of the basic form exist (Frank, Huskamp, McGuire, and Newhouse, 1996). In the second form of carve-out, the enrollee simply chooses a plan, and once in the plan finds that mental health care is being managed by a carve-out vendor.

It is difficult to know the precise number of people in carve-out plans of each type. Recent reports from Foster-Higgins estimate that 35 percent of employers with over five thousand employees have created payer carve-outs, while only 3 percent of firms with under five hundred employees have chosen to organize their managed mental health care plan in this manner (Umland, 1995). By the end of 1995, twelve states had chosen the payer carve-out approach to managed mental health care for Medicaid enrollees. Several additional states have adopted this approach in the intervening two years. A recent survey of fifty large HMOs reports that approximately 50 percent of the forty-two million enrollees in those plans were enrolled in a health plan subcontract form of mental health carve-out (Oss, Drissel, and Clary, 1997).

The two forms of carve-out arrangements serve very different functions in the market for mental health services.

Behavioral Health Plan Subcontracts and Competitive Health Plans

The health plan subcontract is the simpler form of carve-out, and we begin with that. The payer (an employer, for example) purchases coverage and management of all health risks together from a set of integrated health plans, and does not write a separate contract with a mental health vendor. The employer delegates responsibility for all health care to a set of competitive health plans. Employees and dependents make enrollment choices. The decision to carve out behavioral health is made by the health plan, and it is the health plan that has a contract with the vendor. The available data suggest that specialty subcontracts by health plans (HMOs, POS plans, and PPOs) are a large and growing factor in the delivery of mental health services in managed care. A recent survey of the local HMO plans owned by a large national managed care company that enrolls over 2.2 million people offers a selected profile of the health plan subcontract form of carve-out (Huskamp, Aubert, Frank, and Gazmararian, 1996). The majority of those plans use carve-outs. The carve-out contracts vary considerably with respect to organizational features and risk-contracting features. The results of the survey appear to be consistent with the limited national data that is available (Levin, 1992).

The surveyed vendors indicated that 52 percent of their carve-out enrollees were in programs where the vendor was paid on the basis of full (or pure) capitation, 16 percent used risk-sharing contracts, 12 percent were administrative service organization (ASO) contracts, and 20 percent were budgeted systems. The carve-outs generally organized their clinical services either as pure networks or as group models, with the latter form somewhat more popular, while one plan used a facility-based staff model. All carve-out vendors used a utilization review system for inpatient care. About 50 percent used outpatient utilization review, while most of the other vendors used more arm's-length techniques such as incentive arrangements (bonuses and withholds) and professional profiling. In all cases a high level of specialized mental health and substance abuse expertise was interjected at a number of points in the management and delivery of care.

Why do HMOs and other plans carve out mental health care? Hodgkin, Horgan, and Garnick (1997) propose that carve-outs offer efficiencies derived from specialization of expertise in managed behavioral health. In particular, a specialized vendor may be in a more favorable position than an integrated plan to efficiently identify and contract with behavioral health providers to deliver services, to monitor the costs and quality of care, and to manage the care appropriately. It is likely to incur lower costs to provide a given level of care than the comprehensive plan would pay to provide that care in-house. Better information about treatment and the local market may allow specialized vendors to identify the most qualified and efficient specialty providers, define and measure quality and appropriate utilization, and set out utilization management criteria such as level-of-care guidelines for behavioral health services.

Hodgkin, Horgan, and Garnick (1997) identify a set of factors that when present may offer the carve-out form a cost advantage because of information advantages. These include health plan size, health plan model (for example, IPA versus staff model HMO), and competition in the market for behavioral health services. Network models in managed care delegate much management of care to primary care physicians, medical groups, and affiliated specialists (Kerr and others, 1995). This serves to increase the difficulty and costs of managing and monitoring performance in a specialized area of medicine. These costs may be especially high in the behavioral health area because the mental health system is detached from much of the rest of medicine. Thus, health plans that have been organized with an emphasis on expertise in monitoring and managing networks of primary care medical groups and specialists in medicine and surgery may be unfamiliar with markets for behavioral health care. Identifying providers to create a network, establishing clinical protocols and review procedures, and dealing with some unique legal and regulatory features of behavioral health care may be quite different from the core competencies of many health plans.

Smaller network model health plans may find it excessively costly to create their own expertise in the behavioral health area. In addition, the volume of behavioral health services used by a smaller health plan's members may not leave the health plan sufficient bargaining power to effectively construct a specialty provider network. It may be more efficient and yield better care to rent the necessary expertise from an organization that specializes in management of behavioral health care and handles a sufficiently large volume of cases to be in a strong bargaining position versus its provider network. Finally, as noted earlier, carve-out plans commonly use capitation payments in subcontracting, thereby assigning the financial risk for behavioral health services to a separate organization. This may be especially appealing for an organization that has little expertise in behavioral health and might view entry into the behavioral health field as more risky than its other activities.

Direct Payer Carve-Outs for Behavioral Health Care

In a direct payer carve-out the payer (employer) separates part of the health risk from the overall insurance plan and contracts to have it managed by a specialty behavioral health care organization. Enrollees thus face a choice among competing health plans for most of their health care but are required to join a specialized health plan for behavioral health care. The behavioral health carve-out plan is selected by the payer and all enrollees must join. The presence of a direct payer form of carve-out serves to reduce choice, in the sense that health plans will not be permitted to compete for enrollees on the basis of the quality and cost of behavioral health services. The rationale for this form of organization lies in the desire to eliminate competition among plans to select low-risk enrollees.

Incentives to enroll good risks derive from asymmetry of information between health plans and potential enrollees. Enrollees differ in the degree of risk (that is, in their underlying propensity to use mental health care). If these differences are not reflected by the premium paid to the health plan and enrollees are aware of the differences, health plans have an incentive to structure benefits and to manage care so as to be unattractive to high-cost enrollees and attractive to low-cost enrollees. Since plans wish to be attractive to one class of potential enrollees and not to another, the issue is one of the relative quality of different types of services, not the overall quality of the plan. Thus the quality of some services (those used by good risks) will be too high relative to the "efficient level"—and the quality of others (those used more intensively by bad risks) will be too low. These are the market dynamics that result in the frequently heard observation that "one cannot afford to be the good mental health plan." These forces may be more powerful for mental health than for other types of services.

Individuals can predict their own future need for mental health services better than plans can (Ellis, 1985; Frank, Glazer, and McGuire, 1997). People expecting to use many mental health services will tend to join plans that offer generous coverage, good access, and high-quality mental health and substance abuse care. Users of mental health services are poor risks, using more of other health services as well as mental health. Data on Medicaid enrollees in Michigan show that over a three-year period individuals who used mental health services cost an average of $3,722 in health care compared to $1,873 for the average enrollee. Approximately 63 percent of the difference was due to higher levels of mental health care, but the costs of other health care were also higher.

Several studies have provided evidence on adverse selection in health plans. Ellis (1985) showed that a history of mental health spending had a significant influence on individuals' choice of health plan. Higher levels of prior-year spending on mental health care increase the likelihood that an individual will choose more generous coverage. Deb, Rubin, Wilcox-Gök, and Holmes (1996) offer evidence indicating that individuals with a family member with a mental illness are more likely to choose health plans with generous mental health provisions. A recent study from Switzerland by Perneger, Allaz, Etter, and Rougemont (1995) examined health plan choice between an indemnity insurance plan and a managed care plan. They found that individuals with a history of mental health care utilization were significantly more likely than otherwise similar enrollees to choose the indemnity insurance plan. Together, these studies show that users of mental health care will systematically choose plans offering them more generous terms for receiving mental health care—placing those plans at a financial disadvantage. Thus plans have a strong incentive to avoid being attractive to individuals with elevated risks of using mental health services.

The direct payer form of carve-out can reduce competition for the good risks. Carving out the benefit in a separate contract effectively eliminates competition to avoid the high users of mental health care. This is accomplished by separating the behavioral health care budget in a carve-out contract and then reducing the choice of enrollees with respect to the plan that provides mental health services.

Payers reorient competition by choosing a behavioral carve-out for their mental health and substance abuse risk. Competition for enrollees continues among health plans, yet behavioral health services are removed from the calculus of enrollment strategies adopted by plans. Competition for behavioral health service is confined to competition for the carve-out contract. The payer sets out purchasing specifications that are incorporated in a Request for Proposals (RFP) from qualified potential vendors. The RFP details the benefit design, financial risk-sharing arrangements, performance standards for access and quality of care, and historical spending on behavioral health care of the population. Typically, four to ten vendors bid on contracts for larger population groups. The managed behavioral health care (MBHC) industry remains quite competitive with five to seven large national vendors and another twenty to thirty smaller national and regional vendors of behavioral health services (Oss, Drissel, and Clary, 1997; Huskamp, Aubert, Frank, and Guzmararian, 1996). The purpose of competition for MBHC contracts is to limit contract costs and elicit commitments to adhere to certain standards that can be written into a contract. Contracts are typically renewed competitively after two to three years, which requires incumbent vendors to compete with other firms to retain the contract. A number of large purchasers have recently switched vendors when they have been dissatisfied with the performance of their MBHC contract (for example, the Ohio and Massachusetts state governments, and IBM).

Discussion

Specialized behavioral health carve-out arrangements have become a common feature defining the delivery and management of mental health and substance abuse treatment in the United States. We have identified two main classes of carve-out contracts, the health plan subcontract and the direct payer carve-out. Both types of contracts offer potential gains in efficiency due to specialized knowledge and expertise in mental health and substance abuse treatment. Because behavioral health care and general medical care have historically evolved along parallel but largely separate tracks, it is common for health plans to lack specialized skill in the management and delivery of mental health and substance abuse care. The special expertise of MBHC vendors thereby offers health plans and payers the opportunity to rent expertise. This is a common benefit offered by both forms of carve-out.

While the MBHC vendors that enter into each type of contract are the same, however, the economic functions of the two contractual forms are quite different. The health plan specialty subcontract is the result of a health plan's choice given that it must compete for enrollees across all risks. The health plan must therefore take into account the impact on enrollment of the specific features of its behavioral health program. Thus the impact on enrollment of benefit package design, ease of access to behavioral health services, and the quality of those services will be taken into account when a carve-out vendor is selected. Incentives to avoid bad risks will be present and will almost certainly influence the implementation of the carve-out program. Hence the resources devoted to the subcontract, the level of management requested, and the performance standards required will reflect the competition for enrollees among health plans.

The direct payer form of carve-out offers efficiencies of specialization as well. However, because behavioral health is removed from health plan competition, the benefit features, access, and quality of mental health and substance abuse care are likely to be quite different from what is found in the typical health plan subcontract form of carve-out. Direct payer carve-outs offer the added benefit of increased efficiency stemming from eliminating risk selection.

Both forms of carve-out involve additional costs. First, carve-outs create new administrative burdens that appear to range from about 8 to 15 percent of behavioral health care costs. Second, there are additional costs for coordination of care. Much controversy remains about whether behavioral health services are more effectively delivered by specialty providers or by having the primary care physician serve as the coordinator of both general medical and mental health services. All agree that coordination of care is beneficial, but it remains unclear whether primary practitioners will appropriately identify and whether they can effectively coordinate behavioral health care and substance abuse services (Schulberg and Manderscheid, 1989).

References

Bureau of Labor Statistics. *Employer Benefit Survey*. Unpublished data, 1995.

Deb, P., Rubin, J., Wilcox-Gök, V., and Holmes, A. "Choice of Health Insurance by Families of the Mentally Ill." *Health Economics*, 1996, 5, 61–76.

Ellis, R. P. "The Effect of prior year health expenditures on health coverage plan choice." In R. Scheffler and L. Rossiter (eds.), *Advances in Health Economics and Health Services Research*. Greenwich, Conn.: JAI Press, 1985.

Frank, R. G., Glazer, J., and McGuire, P. G. "Measuring Adverse Selection in Managed Health Care." Working paper, Boston University, Nov. 1997.

Frank, R. G., Huskamp, H. A., McGuire, T. G., and Newhouse, J. P. "Some Economics of Mental Health Carve-Outs." *Archives of General Psychiatry*, 1996, 53, 933–937.

Hodgkin, D., Horgan, C. M., and Garnick, D. W. "Make or Buy: HMOs' Contracting Arrangements for Mental Health Care." *Administration and Policy in Mental Health*, 1997, 24, 359–376.

Huskamp, H. A., Aubert, R., Frank, R. G., and Gazmararian, J. "Behavioral Health Carve-Outs in Managed Care." Working paper, Harvard University, 1996.

Kerr, I. A., Mittman, B. S., Hays, R. D., Brooks, R., and others. "Managed Care and Capitation in California: How Do Physicians at Financial Risk Control Their Own Utilization?" *Annals of Internal Medicine*, 1995, 123, 500–504.

Levin, B. L. "Mental Health Services Within the HMOs Group." *HMO*, 1992, 6, 16–21.

Oss, M. E., Drissel, A. B., and Clary, J. *Managed Behavioral Health Market Share in the United States, 1997–1998*. Gettysburg, Pa.: OPEN MINDS, 1997.

Perneger, T. V., Allaz, A. F., Etter, J. F., and Rougemont, A. "Mental Health and Choice Between Managed Care and Indemnity Health Insurance." *American Journal of Psychiatry*, 1995, 52, 1020–1025.

Schulberg, H. C., and Manderscheid, R. W. In C. A. Taube, D. Mechanic, and A. Hohmann (eds.), *The Future of Mental Health Services Research*. DHHS pub. no. (ADM) 89–160. Washington, D.C.: U.S. Government Printing Office, 1989.

RICHARD G. FRANK is professor of health economics in the Department of Health Care Policy at Harvard Medical School.

THOMAS G. MCGUIRE is professor of economics in the Department of Economics at Boston University.

PART TWO

Special Issues

Medicaid's embrace of managed care and aggressive purchasing must be employed in a balanced and thoughtful way in serving vulnerable populations.

Medicaid Managed Care for Special Need Populations: Behavioral Health as "Tracer Condition"

Robert E. Hurley, Debra A. Draper

Medicaid managed care has expanded dramatically over the past half-decade, growing from approximately three million enrollees in 1991 to over thirteen million five years later (Health Care Financing Administration, 1997a, 1997b). The growth has been largely concentrated among the relatively healthy women and children in the Medicaid program, whose needs are the most similar to those found in commercial managed care organizations (MCOs), and who represent approximately 70 percent of the Medicaid population. The rate of expansion has been distinctly slower among those special need beneficiaries—the aged, disabled, and chronically ill—whose service requirements are more extensive, complex, and persistent, and who represent about 70 percent of total Medicaid expenditures (Hurley, Kirschner, and Bone, 1997; Somers and Martin, 1997). The reasons for the slower pace are related to greater heterogeneity and diversity among these populations, widely held skepticism about conventional MCO readiness and willingness to serve these persons, and substantial constraints on the ability of Medicaid officials to embrace strategies that may conflict with those of sister state agencies. And looming over much of this activity is a fundamental debate regarding the respective roles of the public and private sectors in health care delivery.

All these factors appear to be affecting the extension of Medicaid managed care to persons with severe and persistent mental illness (SPMI)—a substantial portion of whom have Medicaid eligibility by virtue of their receipt of Supplemental Security Income (SSI) disability benefits. The purchase of behavioral health services for these individuals in a managed care environment has proven exceedingly challenging to state Medicaid officials. The various models and approaches that have been adopted reflect the iterative and opportunistic maneuvering that has characterized much of the managed care era (Faulkner and Gray, 1997; Hurley, Kirschner and Bone, 1997; Riley, Rawlings-Sekunda, and Pernice, 1997; General Accounting Office, 1996; Gold, Sparer, and Chu, 1996; Kaiser Commission on the Future of Medicaid, 1995). Mental illness is rarely found in isolation, as complications and comorbidities add additional health and other human service requirements beyond what behavioral health providers can deliver. Great concern exists about how MCOs can, should, and do deliver an integrated package of services, as many of them are already using capitated subcontractors to render care (Iglehart, 1996; Frank, McGuire, and Newhouse, 1995). Purchasers in turn struggle with the decision to buy mental health benefits through full-service MCOs or to buy these benefits separately from specialized contractors. For public purchasers, the approach to the market is almost certainly going to be shaped and conditioned by the existing public mental health delivery systems that may be enhanced, threatened, or even undermined by new managed care initiatives.

This chapter provides a brief review of the evolution of Medicaid managed care. It describes the general approaches to Medicaid managed care employed by states, and how these models have been adapted and augmented to extend managed care to the behavioral health realm. In the process, it describes both mainstreaming and targeted or carve-out initiatives.

Then it presents a series of distinctive challenges associated with devising behavioral health managed care programs within Medicaid. Throughout the presentation, the experience with behavioral health is linked to the broader complexities that Medicaid faces as managed care approaches are extended to the many special need populations for whom the states purchase and guarantee health benefits.

Background

The rapid and pervasive expansion of Medicaid managed care has been well documented (Health Care Financing Administration, 1997a; Hurley, Kirschner, and Bone, 1997). Like its private sector counterpart, Medicaid managed care can be construed as a buyer's revolution: a revolution in pursuit of better value from providers of care. The familiar formulation for value of outcome over cost suggests that buyers can obtain greater value by holding outcomes constant and lowering costs, improving outcomes while holding costs constant, or some combination of change in both the numerator and denominator. In general, given Medicaid's well-earned reputation as the most penurious of purchasers, value enhancement via substantial cost reduction has been difficult. Credible reported savings typically are in the 5 percent to 10 percent range among the Aid to Families with Dependent Children/Temporary Assistance to Needy Families (AFDC/TANF) population (Kaiser Commission on the Future of Medicaid, 1995; Hurley, Freund, and Paul, 1993). Cost savings could possibly be greater among SSI beneficiaries, but the only well-substantiated evidence to date on this issue comes from one state, Arizona (McCall, 1997; McCall, Wrightson, Paringer, and Trapnell, 1994).

Improving outcomes presents equally daunting challenges, in part because of all the usual measurement difficulties and complexities. But from a purchaser standpoint, Medicaid administrators suggest that one of the most significant outcome enhancements to date is improved accountability in care. This is achieved by having a single point of contact with which they contract and whose performance they can systematically monitor. In addition, they gain increased predictability in future costs because they can shift the risk for changes in volume and price inflation onto prepaid MCOs with future rate increases subject to negotiation or fiat. Both these gains presuppose that the adopted form of managed care is a prepaid model—which still only accounts for about one-half of all the Medicaid managed care participants in the nation (Health Care Financing Administration, 1997b).

Enrolling beneficiaries in capitated MCOs can be viewed as an example of privatizing the Medicaid program—one beneficiary at a time (Hurley, forthcoming). This assertion underscores how much of the judgment and discretion about actual care delivery is delegated, in effect, to private contractors who themselves have created their own customized delivery systems through what Rosenbaum calls a "series of cascading contracts" (Rosenbaum, Shin, Smith, and Wehr, 1997). Some of the most serious challenges that Medicaid managed care presents to state agencies revolve around how to effectively engineer this use of private contractors without relinquishing statutory responsibility and operational accountability for what happens to beneficiaries. The evidence suggests that there has been enormous variation in how demanding states have chosen to be, and in the specificity with which they have crafted and executed contracts (Faulkner and Gray, 1997; Hurley, Kirschner, and Bone, 1997; Riley, Rawlings-Sekunda, and Pernice, 1997; General Accounting Office, 1996; Gold, Sparer, and Chu, 1996; Kaiser Commission on the Future of Medicaid, 1995). There may be even greater variability in the rigor of state-MCO contract enforcement.

This transformation of the Medicaid program to aggressive, sophisticated purchaser on behalf of its enrollees—the prototypical role for the buyer in the managed care revolution—is not without some inevitable conflicts, because Medicaid has been assigned or has assumed a number of supplemental roles. These include serving as a safe-guardian and financier of safety-net providers for uninsured persons, as a largely passive conduit of funding for key health and human services provided by other state agencies as well as some private organizations, as a source of substantial subsidies for medical education, and as an articulator and advocate for rights and right-to-services for selected vulnerable populations. One of the discoveries that many private MCOs have made as they entered the Medicaid line of business is that the ambivalent and erratic purchasing approach often taken by Medicaid agencies can make operating as their agent very difficult. Efforts to extend managed care to populations with special needs seems to have brought many of these conflicts into sharp focus.

Managed Care in the Medicaid Program

Medicaid agencies have embraced three broad models of managed care to obtain acute physical health services for beneficiaries: fee-for-service primary care case management (PCCM), partial capitation or less-than-full-risk programs, and full-risk capitation with prepaid managed care organizations (Hurley, Freund, and Paul, 1993). There are many variants of these basic models, and states often employ combinations to adapt their strategies to local market conditions and readiness (National Academy for State Health Policy, 1997). In recent years the trend has been toward full-risk capitation arrangements, made possible by the proliferation of health maintenance organizations (HMOs) and their spread from major urban to small and mid sized communities and even into some rural areas. Paralleling this development has been the growing preference of states for mandatory enrollment, primarily for the AFDC/TANF population. Such approaches allow states to avoid the favorable selection enjoyed by MCOs in voluntary programs, which undermined cost savings possibilities. Consequently, this permits them to get the desirable financial risk shifting to MCOs that improves future cost predictability.

Typically, these approaches have had a very limited impact on behavioral health services, an outcome attributable both to the population covered and to the way the programs were structured. The use of behavioral health services by the general AFDC/TANF population has been very low, and thus shifts in their care would have had negligible effects on providers. With respect to models, PCCM programs pay primary care physicians to provide or authorize all medical services, but this model is, at best, a minimalist approach to managed care. For persons receiving behavioral health services, these models may impose a requirement that such care be authorized by the case manager or gatekeeper—though some states have exempted behavioral health from such authorization, actually anticipating what has now become a public clamor for direct access. Anecdotal evidence suggests that voluntary enrollment in risk programs has been low among SSI beneficiaries who have chronic mental illness—though there have been reports that they may have been targets for active recruitment by unscrupulous marketers at one time, before most states clamped down on direct marketing and enrollment by MCOs (Gold, Sparer, and Chu, 1996).

These experiences are similar to those of other special need populations such as persons with developmental disabilities or severe physical disabilities, or with disabling or degenerative chronic illnesses such as HIV/AIDS, whose exposure to Medicaid managed care has been delayed, deferred, or diluted (General Accounting Office, 1996). For some of these persons, specialized programs have been facilitated through the use of the home- and community-based waiver authority granted to states by the Health Care Financing Administration (HCFA). In a number of instances, certain members of these populations have been exempted from participation in mandatory programs or excluded from voluntary enrollment because of serious administrative complexities that impede enrollment in capitated models—dual eligibility for Medicaid and Medicare or institutionalized status providing two of the best examples. In a few cases, efforts have been undertaken to design specialized programs or models that target one or more of the highly heterogeneous subgroups with SSI eligibility to offer customized arrangements with some managed care properties. These include capitation with full risk or perhaps risk-sharing arrangements between programs and Medicaid agencies. Such programs have typically been slow to develop and limited in their attraction of both providers and enrollees. This lack of progress reflects administrative, economic, clinical, and cultural impediments that require further discussion after introducing the particular challenges of managed behavioral health in Medicaid.

Managed Behavioral Health in the Medicaid Program

Even if persons with chronic illness were never enrolled in Medicaid managed care arrangements, Medicaid administrators would ultimately have had to deal with how to make their embrace of managed care compatible with larger changes in behavioral health in general, and publicly financed and delivered behavioral health in particular. The profound impact of managed care on behavioral health has arguably been the most traumatic manifestation of the buyers' revolution. Pressures seem to be unabated in terms of addressing both outcomes and costs in this field, as buyers seek to establish what works and eliminate what doesn't. Few service providers in the private and public sector have escaped this maelstrom of change. Demands have grown for lower-priced services, improved performance data, increased accountability for outcomes, and a careful reappraisal of the appropriateness of an entire spectrum of services that have historically been perceived as being of value. And the rise of commercial entities to play this rationalizer and challenger role has injected further controversy and contention over whether they are value-adders or reducers.

Public mental health systems have not been spared these pressures. Their eagerness to diversify revenue sources has increased their vulnerability and subjected them to unfamiliar competitive pressures and managed care practices at an expanding pace. Ironically, access to public sector resources has improved in recent years as many of these public agencies gained access to Medicaid revenues through what some would characterize as creative financing and accounting methods in state government to maximize federal Medicaid match. Others might call it an example of states, in effect, being allowed to borrow the federal credit card—at least for a time. In addition, public providers have been encouraged to obtain Medicaid fee-for-service provider status and bill directly for covered services for which Medicaid has already been paying private providers.

Mainstreaming Versus Targeted Approaches. As Medicaid agencies embraced managed care, it was necessary to address how new models would provide behavioral health services including not only from and for whom they would buy, but what they would buy as well. Bachman and Burwell (1997) describe the two principal approaches in use as mainstream and carve-out arrangements and indicate how these approaches have been meshed with the alternative models of physical health managed care employed by states. The mainstream approach in prepaid models includes payments for behavioral health within the capitated premium paid to an MCO. This grants that entity the flexibility to decide if it wishes to provide these services directly or in turn to subcontract with a specialized provider for them. If states operate a PCCM program there are likely to be few changes in access to and delivery of behavioral health services, except for the authorization process previously described. In both approaches, the implications for AFDC/TANF beneficiaries are minimal since capitation payments include a very modest behavioral health component and the level of utilization of behavioral health services tends to be quite low for both models (Bachman and Burwell, 1997). Thus little attention was given to behavioral health matters in the first generation of Medicaid managed care.

Private purchasing of behavioral health services increasingly promoted managed care models in the late 1980s and early 1990s, widening the exposure of all providers to these emergent arrangements. New models explicitly separated the buying of behavioral health from physical health services. Even fully capitated MCOs subcontract for these services with private behavioral health companies (Frank, Huskamp, McGuire, and Newhouse, 1996; Frank, McGuire, and Newhouse, 1995). The rise of these companies and their burgeoning provider networks presented both opportunities and challenges for Medicaid agencies to buy behavioral health services separately or, as Bachman and Burwell (1997) describe it, on a more targeted basis. Medicaid agencies could directly contract with private behavioral health companies on a fixed-price basis and gain savings and, at least in theory, more accountability. Alternatively, they could encourage or induce full-service MCOs to subcontract for mental health services with the behavioral health companies. The inherent challenge to this approach was the possibility that the provider networks might not include public sector or other traditional Medicaid providers or, if they did so, they might not provide sufficiently generous compensation to assure the survival of the traditional providers. Not only might this reduce the quality of services to Medicaid beneficiaries, it might also reduce it for persons without insurance whose care may have been cross-subsidized in part by Medicaid payments. A growing number of public providers, publicly sponsored community mental health officials, and state mental health agency officials began to advocate for both the proverbial "seat at the table" in program design and for specific accommodations to preserve and protect the ostensibly jeopardized safety net (Andrulis, 1997; Baxter and Mechanic, 1997; Dallek, 1996; Lipson, 1997; Lipson and Naierman, 1996).

Carve-Out Arrangements. Initially these accommodations included service carve-outs—where certain existing arrangements were maintained by not subjecting them to managed care administration or terms. These models sometimes included requirements that community mental health authorities be given preferred status in contracting, occasionally with a first-right-of-refusal to be the capitated carve-out provider. In other cases, private contracts were mandated to incorporate certain essential community providers—public and private—into their networks to allow them to maintain access to revenue streams. But typically, physical health care was provided to these persons through the adopted Medicaid managed care model that was in place in the particular state or locality. Some states went beyond this with population carve-outs because of concerns about fragmentation of care or where existing customized case management models had already been molded and could be undermined by changes in financial or provider arrangements (Bachman and Burwell, 1997).

The stakes associated with Medicaid managed care for behavioral health increased dramatically when states began to move SSI beneficiaries into managed care arrangements—especially fully capitated arrangements—on a mandatory basis. Though SSI beneficiaries include many heterogeneous groups, persons with SPMI represent one of the largest components and they became a natural focus for population carve-out models. With substantially greater service needs—and thus expected costs—the portion of the capitation rate attributable to behavioral health services is markedly higher, and many purchasers have chosen not to include these additional costs in their capitation payment to MCOs. Also, many persons with SPMI receive their medications, maintenance services, and other therapies through publicly sponsored community mental health services—some of which have been financed already with Medicaid fee-for-service billings. State and local officials became concerned about the potential loss or diversion of these funds. Finally, many of the advocacy groups representing persons with SPMI have been suspicious of the methods, motives, and commitment of commercial behavioral health companies with regard to this population.

Specialized Plans. In addition to adding impetus to the movement for population carve-outs, another of Bachman and Burwell's targeted strategies—the specialized plan—has found fertile ground in some states and locales where sentiment has supported creating capitated models for the SPMI. These models, some of which are described in detail elsewhere in this sourcebook, have numerous manifestations but commonly attempt to position plans or organizations having special expertise with persons with SPMI to play the lead role in clinical and financial management of services. In some instances, they even reverse the capitation and subcapitation roles between physical and behavioral health contractors. In other instances, they attempt to devise customized care management entities that are centered on a behavioral health system that provides, buys, or facilitates the purchase of all health services for enrollees. Such models are also said to offer the promise of bringing in other funding streams to which these entities may have access but which Medicaid does not finance on a fee-for-service basis, such as residential care or vocational rehabilitation (Bachman and Burwell,

1997). Development of such models demands concerted alignment of efforts and resources between state and local officials and among state agencies, many of whom have a far broader clientele than Medicaid beneficiaries.

Simply summarizing these models and tracing their origins illustrates some of the complexities Medicaid agencies face as they attempt to expand managed care to groups with more intensive and chronic needs, which is where the bulk of the Medicaid budget is expended. The pace of implementation has been very slow in part because early efforts to move into these areas encountered resistance based on ignorance, indifference, or denial with respect to managed care and its likely implications. Resistance has now become more informed, purposeful, and strategic as the major stakeholders come to recognize the truly revolutionizing potential of a predominantly managed care–based Medicaid program. Likewise, Medicaid agencies themselves have discovered and accepted encumbrances that are self-inflicted given their own multiple, conflicting roles and their often ambivalent attitudes toward doing the public's business through private contractors. These observations transcend the behavioral health realm as indicated in the following discussion of some specific challenges associated with managed care for special need populations.

Medicaid Managed Care and Special Need Purchasing: Common Themes

The challenges of developing behavioral health managed care initiatives in Medicaid manifest the same underlying difficulties for Medicaid agencies with multiple and complex roles that are being encountered for many other vulnerable population subgroups with special needs. Several of these challenges are described to demonstrate just how behavioral health is a kind of tracer condition that both merits study in its own right and also because it reveals other broader transformations occurring in the health care marketplace.

Specialness and Mainstreaming. Like much of the terminology of the managed care movement, the terms *specialness* and *mainstreaming* are ill-defined and loosely used. Both demand more precise definition so that the issues often glossed over in discussion will receive needed reflection and resolution.

Specialness is often associated with descriptions of disabling conditions. But it is a multidimensional term that needs to be modified or qualified in a number of ways. For example, it is necessary to consider how permanent a condition is, how comprehensive it may be, how much it is self-asserted or self-acknowledged, how recognized or accepted it is by others, how discrete or subject to confounding by comorbidities or complications it is, and how narrow or broad it is in its implication for service use (Hurley and Draper, forthcoming; LaPlante, 1991; West, 1991). For some persons, specialness implies a need for or entitlement to a wide spectrum of distinctive services and accommodations necessary to ensure access to appropriate care. For others, the basis for specialness can be approached on a targeted basis to ensure access and also to minimize disruption to the remainder of a population. Both these approaches can be used to promote the development of specialized plans for persons with SPMI as they have been for those with other disabilities.

Mainstreaming has similar connotations and conundrums associated with it (Hurley and Draper, forthcoming). Separate and specialized programs may imply that care will be more suitably customized and individualized, but this may only apply to a number of persons with special needs or to some idiosyncratic service needs. For others, the segregation or separation of special populations may have adverse implications from clinical, economic, and equity vantage points. Persons with some special needs may neither require nor benefit from totally separate delivery systems because their special conditions are not so consuming or all encompassing as to provide adequate justification for segregation. Programs for very small subpopulations may lack the scale and administrative wherewithal to be self-contained and thus are usually not viable. However, in some instances compartmentalizing a limited set of specialized services while promoting access to mainstream services for all other benefits is both economically prudent and socially adaptive for persons with special needs. Such arrangements may avoid exposure to subtle or direct discrimination that infringes on their civil and human rights. Based on this logic, persons with SPMI may benefit from being able to obtain their physical health services from large, established mainstream MCOs. Similar arguments have been advanced for persons with developmental or serious physical disabilities.

Capitation. How great a liberator is capitation? Proponents of managed care for persons with specialness have touted the idea that prepaid managed care affords service providers and managers an opportunity to liberate themselves and their clients and patients from many of the encumbrances of categorically based programs and fragmented fee-for-service financing (Kronick, Zhou, and Dreyfus, 1995; Kronick, Dreyfus, Lee, and Zhou, 1996). Support for attaining this nirvana of seamlessness is widespread in theory, but much less widespread in practice. Some of this reticence seems grounded in concerns about the potential inducements offered by capitation to underserve clients, especially if the capitated entities themselves are not carefully selected. More generally, the concerns about capitation typically reflect a recognition that for prepaid care to be effective and suitable for persons with substantial costs or high probabilities of use, the rates paid must be both adequate and appropriately adjusted (General Accounting Office, 1996; Kronick, Dreyfus, Lee, and Zhou, 1996; Frank, McGuire, and Newhouse, 1995).

The real danger of inadequate risk adjustment is that MCOs receive a clear signal to, in essence, get good but not too good—because excelling in care for special need populations may result in attracting a disproportionate number of enrollees for whom services may be systematically underfinanced. While help may be on the way in terms of new methodologies, some states have either moved ahead without these protections (for both MCOs and beneficiaries) or introduced risk corridors to safeguard all parties (General Accounting Office, 1996). Further limitations of capitation have been revealed in carve-out and subcapitation models, where narrowly defined scopes of services and payment arrangements may be administratively feasible or even desirable, but may not be well aligned with processes of service delivery. Thus cases of discrete payments for indistinct needs clash when patients (or clients, or members—the names vary) find that capitation payments may create rough, insurmountable seams rather than seamlessness (Hurley and Draper, forthcoming). For example, pharmacy benefits may be incorporated in and paid via a physical health capitation but the prescription may be ordered by a clinician from a subcapitated behavioral health organization, thereby setting the stage for conflicts and disputes between capitation holders.

Beyond the Medical Model. While managed care organizations have been characterized by many as alternative financing and delivery systems, in truth they have succeeded largely by emulating or shadowing conventional medical practice. In pursuit of legitimacy and consumer and provider acceptance, they have subscribed to and perpetuated a medical model of care delivery. This adherence to conventional approaches to organizing and rendering services has raised questions as to MCO suitability to serve persons whose needs may not fit well with the acute-care, physician-driven bias found throughout the medical system. Such approaches have come to be viewed as deficient for many chronic physical conditions (Wagner, Austin, and Von Korff, 1996), so extending them to persons with developmental or permanent physical disabilities or long-term behavioral health problems of uncertain etiology produces considerable skepticism, stress, and strain (Mechanic, Schlesinger, and McAlpine, 1995). Familiarity and experience with a far broader array of human services seems a missing prerequisite for success.

These qualms extend not only to the competence and proficiency of clinical personnel but also to the design of benefit packages and flexibility in administering and interpreting coverage. MCOs may adhere to rigid criteria of medical necessity that have not been adapted to address sensitive areas regarding social necessity, palliative treatment, or maintenance care. Duration or scope of treatment restrictions may have to be adjusted to reflect the different prognostic realities associated with treatment of persons with chronic, debilitating conditions. MCOs may also have had few previous opportunities or incentives to contract for certain types of services because of their homogeneous membership, which has had relatively little need for personal care attendants, day treatment programs, residential care, and vocational rehabilitation services of the type needed by people with SPMI.

Reliance on social and other nonmedical human services invariably brings MCOs into contact with public sector providers—most of whom will already have relationships with special need clientele. Often these are local (city or county) agencies that add additional complexity to contracting, which may discourage private plans from participating, or may induce them to seek to develop competing in-house services to avoid some of these complications. Alternatively, in some states such as Arizona, publicly sponsored organizations have become prepaid entities in order to gain or ensure access to revenue streams to support existing structures (Baxter and Mechanic, 1997; Lipson, 1997). Such strategic maneuvering is analogous to that currently being observed among groups of physicians or hospital-based systems seeking to supplant MCOs as the recipient of premium payments from purchasers. There appears to be a growing movement among community mental health agencies to devise a similar strategy and to seek positioning in state policies to gain this first-right-of-refusal status. While a compelling case can be made for this stratagem to preserve core support, public managers still need to be prepared to apply the same make-or-buy decision making that capitation has motivated their private sector counterparts to engage in.

Safety Net Providers in a Managed Care World. These close encounters between public human service organizations and private MCOs underscore the significant threat represented by the growing use of private contractors by Medicaid agencies (Andrulis, 1997; Baxter and Mechanic, 1997; Dallek, 1996; Lipson, 1997; Lipson and Naierman, 1996).

Ironically, one reason Medicaid agencies embrace these contractors appears to be that it may be easier to impose some control over sister state agencies and local officials through a contract with a private third party than through direct negotiation with them. Significant protections have been layered on by legislation and regulation to maintain public service organizations (Hurley, forthcoming). Financial and political pressures and interagency or intergovernmental rivalries may impede direct negotiations and prevent innovation from moving forward. In the case of behavioral health, innovation may be badly hampered by serious concerns about the impact on job security for public employees in institutional settings. Delegating this difficult and delicate work to private contractors may help avoid some of these conflicts. It may distance public officials from responsibility for such developments, and the private contractors may be able to engage in ground-level negotiations with providers without some of the political overtones.

The risk with this approach is that carefully crafted webs of cross-subsidization for service delivery can be disturbed if single-minded, best-priced buying is injected into these systems. Medicaid dollars—both from billings and from state-level matching schemes—are not only critical for care to Medicaid beneficiaries, they are also often integral to maintaining the capacity of provider organizations to serve persons without coverage. Thus rapid and sustained withdrawal of these funds can contribute to the implosion of service delivery systems and, in particular, of public service providers, who typically enjoy the dubious distinction of being providers of last resort and experiencing the corresponding adverse selection that the title implies (Andrulis, 1997; Baxter and Mechanic, 1997; Gold, Sparer, and Chu, 1996; Lipson, 1997; Lipson and Naierman, 1996). Concern about this collision course seems to be growing as the zest for privatization of public services spreads at a faster pace than enthusiasm for universal health insurance coverage (Baxter and Mechanic, 1997). The expected impact of this collision will be more substantial in special need service areas as the costs of this care and the stakes for not rendering it on a timely, appropriate basis are greater.

Stakeholder Involvement and Influence. The contemporary backlash against many features of managed care resonates with and confirms many of the concerns raised by persons with special needs, who are skeptical of the ability and willingness of commercial HMOs—generic or specialized—to meet their needs. Platitudes about primary prevention and population-based health care ring hollow with persons with chronic, consuming conditions who have relentlessly struggled to craft their own self-managed care system. Family members and advocacy organizations have seized on these concerns and asserted the need for more active involvement, input, and voice in managed care models being customized for new members with distinctive needs that may be unfamiliar to conventional managed care organizations (Dallek, 1996; Gold, Sparer, and Chu, 1996; Mechanic, 1994). Specialized providers have weighed in on this as well, although such activism may be construed as motivated in part by self-preservation instincts (Lipson, 1997; Iglehart, 1996).

Some Medicaid agencies have been willing to extract from private contractors a commitment to make sincere efforts to engage clientele in program development, design, refinement, and even governance. The challenge is to make such involvement substantive rather than merely symbolic—though even the symbolism may be important to initially overcome the pervasive concern that private organizations will be less open and accountable than public agencies have been (Riley, Rawlings-Sekunda, and Pernice, 1997).

States are also exploring how to use market forces to promote more and better beneficiary education, and to induce members to choose plans that can demonstrate superior performance rather than simply to remain with familiar and traditional providers and delivery systems (Riley, Rawlings-Sekunda, and Pernice, 1997; Gold, Sparer, and Chu, 1996).

Looming Culture Clashes and Values Conflicts

The discussion of specific themes that challenge managed care for special need populations illustrates that continued movement in this direction will be challenging for all parties involved, and the pace of progress will and should be slow and intermittent. In part this is necessary because there are many latent value conflicts that will surface as the numbers and heterogeneity of participants grow and it will take time to achieve resolution. The spread of the commercial ethos into most facets of health services imposes a return-on-investment standard as to what private organizations choose to provide or finance. This standard may promote efficiency and innovation, but its impact on compassionate care and maintenance services is far less certain or sanguine. Building provider networks from among those willing to accept and adopt innovation has considerable surface appeal, but it may lead to limited involvement by those who have demonstrated long-term commitment to serving special need groups that remain unconvinced of the value of change or simply lack the resources to invest in innovation.

Persons with special needs will remain reluctant to embrace models that disrupt established relationships, create daunting risk-sharing or risk-shifting dynamics, or fail to assure them that the same comprehensive range of services they believed they had in a fee-for-service environment will remain available. The fact that these models may save money for payers or may entail lower out-of-pocket costs to enrollees—the motivators that have contributed to dramatic growth in commercial and Medicare managed care—may be of little or no relevance for persons whose cost-participation has been negligible, or whose price sensitivity may be muted because of the consuming nature of their condition or disability. They may also be extremely suspicious of the short-term time horizon of investor-owned enterprises when they contrast this with their own lifelong struggle with a chronic condition.

Medicaid agencies will be at the center of these conflicts and will bear a major responsibility for assuaging these concerns and for keeping the culture clashes under control. Because managed care is a buyers' revolution, this is where the locus of responsibility should lie. There is evidence that Medicaid agencies are becoming more sophisticated purchasers who are improving the skills and instruments needed to extract better value from their contractors in the managed care realm, though the range of variability among states remains a real cause for concern (Rosenbaum, Shin, Smith, and Wehr, 1997). However, because Medicaid agencies have been saddled with several additional responsibilities beyond just getting better value for their covered lives via managed care, as they succeed on that score they are likely to provoke tension and conflict with some of their other roles, and with sister agencies who share responsibilities for meeting the special needs of vulnerable populations.

Conclusion

Medicaid managed care for behavioral health services has advanced at an uneven pace with diverse models and with still uncertain impacts. This assessment applies to most of the Medicaid experience with managed care for populations whose needs are not common, and contrasts with the situation for acute care, for which conventional managed care organizations seem to be generally well suited. Consequently, these models are still going through a kind of shake-down cruise when it comes to their ability to accommodate special need groups and to achieve equal or superior outcomes to the delivery systems they seek to displace. Medicaid's adoption of managed care models for these purposes has significant appeal given the overall apparent success of managed care arrangements to dramatically reduce cost inflation for private purchasers. But the fact that Medicaid has been an integral source of support for many other initiatives and endeavors in the health and human services arenas means that its embrace of the aggressive self-interested buying that managed care represents must be employed in a balanced and thoughtful manner.

References

Andrulis, D. "The Public Sector in Health Care: Evolution or Dissolution." *Health Affairs*, 1997, *16*, 131–140.

Bachman, S., and Burwell, B. *Medicaid Carve-Outs: Policy and Programmatic Considerations.* Princeton, N.J.: Center for Health Care Strategies, 1997.

Baxter, R., and Mechanic, R. "The Status of Local Health Care Safety Nets." *Health Affairs*, 1997, *16*, 7–23.

Dallek, G. "A Consumer Advocate on Medicaid Managed Care." *Health Affairs,* 1996, *15,* 174–177.

Faulkner and Gray. "States Find No Easy Answers on Medicaid Behavioral Care." In R. Cunningham (ed.), *Medicine & Health Perspectives,* June 2, 1997.

Frank, R. G., Huskamp, H. A., McGuire, T. G., and Newhouse, J. P. "Some Economics of Mental Health Carve-Outs." *Archives of General Psychiatry,* 1996, *53,* 933–937.

Frank, R. G., McGuire, T. G., and Newhouse, J. P. "Risk Contracts in Managed Mental Health Care." *Health Affairs,* 1995, *14,* 50–64.

General Accounting Office. *Medicaid Managed Care: Serving the Disabled Challenges States.* (HEHS-96–136). Washington, D.C.: U.S. General Accounting Office, 1996.

Gold, M. R., Sparer, M., and Chu, K. "Medicaid Managed Care: Lessons from Five States." *Health Affairs,* 1996, *15,* 153–166.

Health Care Financing Administration. "Fact Sheet: Managed Care on Medicare and Medicaid." Washington, D.C.: Health Care Financing Administration, Jan. 1997a.

Health Care Financing Administration. *National Summary of Medicaid Managed Care Programs and Enrollment.* Washington, D.C.: Health Care Financing Administration, 1997b.

Hurley, R. "Have We Overdosed on a Panacea: Reflections on the Evolution of Medicaid Managed Care." In S. Somers and S. Davidson (eds.), *Remaking Medicaid: Managed Care for the Public Good.* San Francisco: Jossey-Bass, forthcoming.

Hurley, R., and Draper, D. "Special Plans for Special Persons: The Elusive Pursuit of Customized Managed Care." In S. Somers and S. Davidson (eds.), *Remaking Medicaid: Managed Care for the Public Good.* San Francisco: Jossey-Bass, forthcoming.

Hurley, R., Freund, D., and Paul, J. *Managed Care in Medicaid: Lessons for Policy and Program Design.* Ann Arbor, Mich.: Health Administration Press, 1993.

Hurley, R., Kirschner, L., and Bone, T. "Medicaid Managed Care." In P. Kongstvedt (ed.), *Essentials of Managed Health Care.* (2nd ed.) Gaithersburg, Md.: Aspen, 1997.

Iglehart, J. K. "Health Policy Report: Managed Care and Mental Health." *New England Journal of Medicine,* 1996, *334,* 131–135.

Kaiser Commission on the Future of Medicaid. *Medicaid and Managed Care: Lessons from the Literature.* Menlo Park, Calif.: Kaiser Family Foundation, 1995.

Kronick, R., Dreyfus, T., Lee, L., and Zhou, Z. "Diagnostic Risk Adjustment for Medicaid: The Disability Payment System." *Health Care Financing Review,* 1996, *17,* 7–33.

Kronick, R., Zhou, Z., and Dreyfus, T. "Making Risk Adjustment Work for Everyone." *Inquiry,* 1995, *32,* 41–55.

LaPlante, M. "The Demographics of Disability." *Milbank Quarterly,* 1991, *69*(Suppl.), 55–77.

Lipson, D. "Medicaid Managed Care and Community Providers: New Partnerships." *Health Affairs,* 1997, *16,* 91–107.

Lipson, D., and Naierman, N. "Effects of Health System Changes on Safety Net Providers." *Health Affairs,* 1996, *15,* 33–48.

McCall, N. "Lessons from Arizona's Medicaid Managed Care Program." *Health Affairs,* 1997, *16,* 194–199.

McCall, N., Wrightson, C., Paringer, L., and Trapnell, G. "Managed Medicaid Cost Savings: The Arizona Experience." *Health Affairs,* 1994, *13,* 234–245.

Mechanic, D., Schlesinger, M., and McAlpine, D. "Management of Mental Health and Substance Abuse Services: State of the Art and Early Results." *Milbank Quarterly,* 1995, *73,* 19–55.

Mechanic, D. "Establishing Mental Health Priorities." *Milbank Quarterly,* 1994, *72,* 501–514.

National Academy for State Health Policy. *Medicaid Managed Care: Guide for the States.* (3rd ed.) Portland, Maine: National Academy for State Health Policy, 1997.

Riley, T., Rawlings-Sekunda, J., and Pernice, C. *Transitioning to Managed Care: Medicaid Managed Care in Mental Health.* Kaiser-HCFA State Symposia Series. Portland, Maine: National Academy for State Health Policy, 1997.

Rosenbaum, S., Shin, P., Smith, B., and Wehr, E. *Negotiating the New Health Care System: An Analysis of Contracts Between State Medicaid Agencies and Managed Care Organizations.*

Washington, D.C.: Center for Health Policy Research, George Washington University Medical Center, 1997.

Somers, S., and Martin, R. "Key Issue to Address in Medicaid Managed Care's Future: Populations with Special Needs." In C. Gearon (ed.), *Managed Medicare and Medicaid: Facts, Trends and Data.* Washington, D.C.: Atlantic Information Services, 1997.

Wagner, E., Austin, B., and Von Korff, M. "Organizing Care for Patients with Chronic Illness." *Milbank Quarterly,* 1996, *74,* 511–544.

West, J. "The Social and Policy Context of the Act." *Milbank Quarterly,* 1991, *69*(Suppl.), 3–24.

ROBERT E. HURLEY is an associate professor in the Department of Health Administration at the Medical College of Virginia campus of Virginia Commonwealth University.

DEBRA A. DRAPER is a research assistant and doctoral student in the Department of Health Administration at the Medical College of Virginia campus of Virginia Commonwealth University.

Quality of care can be defined, measured, and improved but the tools available for quality assurance and improvement in mental health and substance abuse are less fully developed and more difficult to apply, especially in the managed care arena.

Quality Assurance in Behavioral Health

Kathleen N. Lohr, William E. Schlenger, J. William Luckey

The Institute of Medicine defines quality of care as "the degree to which health services for individuals and populations increase the likelihood of desired health outcomes and are consistent with current professional knowledge" (1990, p. 21). Although this is not the only definition available, it is a productive one because it points to several significant elements of health care quality and because these elements can be cast into operational terms. First, health services should be understood to encompass a broad range of services that affect both physical health and mental and behavioral health. Second, a focus on both individuals and populations or communities is imperative, as is an appreciation of the concerns for both users and nonusers of health care of services; thus, access to care is a critical correlate of high-quality care. Third, the outcomes of health care must encompass a wide range of clinical and biologic endpoints and, especially, health status and functional outcomes.

An orientation to measurement and improvement of health outcomes does not necessarily take precedence over the measurement and improvement of the processes of care. Attention is now given to the need for more and better evidence that links specific processes to identifiable outcomes. Moreover, in some cases, structural measures of the qualifications and characteristics of health professionals, facilities, or systems may also be important as a complement to processes and outcomes (in the tripartite model of structure, process, and outcome first identified by Donabedian [1966, 1980]).

Quality Problems

Technical and interpersonal incompetence, use of unnecessary and inappropriate services, and underuse (or lack of access to) needed and appropriate services are the typical targets of quality measurement and improvement efforts.

Poor performance by practitioners and facilities will be of concern regardless of the type of health care system in place (whether traditional fee-for-service (FFS), tightly managed capitated systems, or anything in between); overuse is typically thought to be of greater concern in FFS settings than in managed care settings and, conversely, underuse is often believed to be the greater issue in managed care. Regardless of the extent to which managed care becomes the dominant way to organize, finance, and deliver health care in this country, most experts believe that these three problem areas will all continue to be of concern (Chassin, 1997) and that managed care cannot be shown always to be either better, or worse, than FFS care (Miller and Luft, 1997).

Quality Assessment and Measurement. The methods for evaluating quality today are well advanced. A considerable bookshelf exists for process-of-care measures for many diagnoses and symptom states (for example, the CONQUEST system supported by the Agency for Health Care Policy and Research [Palmer and Lawthers, 1997]), and more data are available through computer-based systems than ever before. Reliable and valid instruments can be used by patients to assess their own outcomes, and dozens of performance measurement systems are being implemented across the country. Nevertheless, today's tools still tend to be focused more on hospital or other inpatient facilities than on outpatient settings such as physicians' offices, patients' homes, or other ambulatory settings, a fact that has considerable implications for mental health and substance abuse care. Moreover, progress to date in quality assessment methods has been made mainly in an FFS context, so evaluators now have to devise ways to consider the wide variety of managed care approaches and settings. This fact also has significant implications for assessing the adequacy of managed behavioral health care, especially for programs that have been carved out of basic health care plans or insurance coverage. Furthermore, quality assessment techniques have typically focused on aspects of prevention, diagnosis, therapy, or rehabilitation other than those related to mental health or substance abuse care, leaving those fields relatively lacking in off-the-shelf measures.

Quality Assurance and Quality Improvement. Traditional quality assurance (QA) programs have focused on individual practitioners or institutions, stressed meeting a priori standards, and had a regulatory cast. They were often imposed from the outside, and they often used subjective peer review methods involving retrospective case and chart reviews. In the past decade, newer techniques of continuous quality improvement (QI) have spread through the health care sector (Berwick, 1989). They focus on systems of care, not so-called bad apples, emphasize continuous improvement beyond set standards or norms, rely heavily on data-driven problem identification and feedback of information to clinicians and institutions, and are implemented as internal to health care delivery systems and facilities. Little empirical evidence is available to assess the effectiveness of QI techniques for improving clinical processes or patient outcomes, and many experts doubt QI approaches should wholly supplant QA approaches; rather, a multifaceted mix of external and internal programs embracing regulatory and improvement-oriented efforts may be more likely to succeed in maintaining and enhancing the quality of health care in this nation.

Quality of Care for Mental, Emotional, and Behavioral Conditions. Assessing and improving the quality of medical, social, and other services for patients with mental health and substance abuse problems mean facing special challenges. These include demonstrating the effectiveness of behavioral health interventions, enhancing consumer protection, organizing and financing care, preserving the safety net for special populations, and coordinating care in the primary and specialty sectors (Institute of Medicine, 1997). The rest of this chapter identifies high-priority issues and highlights advances in measuring and enhancing the quality of services for patients with these disorders.

Quality Issues and QA/QI Approaches for Mental Health

Special Issues and Challenges. During the 1980s, costs of providing care for mental, emotional, and substance use problems rose dramatically, beyond even the substantial rate of inflation for other health care costs. As costs of care for these disorders rose, so did questions about the effectiveness and appropriateness of these services.

One major approach to managing behavioral health care is to carve out care for psychiatric and substance abuse disorders and manage it separately from other health care. Although the rationale for deciding to manage care for psychiatric and substance use illnesses separately from other health care may be clear, there are important reasons that doing so might not be a good idea. These include the fact that although established specialty systems provide care for patients with these conditions, the reality is that roughly half of the care for those disorders in the United States is provided in primary care settings (Regier and others, 1993). This suggests that primary care plays at least an important role in any system of care for psychiatric and substance use disorders and that, in fact, the primary care setting may be the *best* vehicle for detection of and early intervention in these illnesses.

Additionally, given the substantial comorbidity of psychiatric and substance use disorders with physical illness (for example, coronary heart disease and major depression; liver disease and alcoholism) and the implications of those comorbidities for the treatment of both kinds of diseases, organizational structures that facilitate integration of care may be more effective in addressing patients' multiple needs than structures that divide them. Consequently, some favor the *carve-in* alternative, in which specialty mental health and substance abuse services are established within comprehensive primary care settings and managed along with other health care under a single budget.

Structure. The structure domain includes "the relatively stable characteristics of the providers of care, of the tools and resources that they have at their disposal, and of the physical and organizational settings in which they work" (Donabedian, 1980, p. 81). A primary mechanism for managing mental health care costs is substitution of lower-cost providers. Thus, in managed networks, clinical social workers may be providing care previously provided by physicians. Although such substitution may be beneficial to both patients and providers in many situations, it may also open the door to inferior clinical decisions and inadequate care.

An important step in providing better tools and resources to providers of behavioral health care is the move toward practice guidelines. Practice guidelines provide practitioners and patients with "systematically developed" information about "appropriate health care for specific clinical circumstances" (Institute of Medicine, 1992, p. 2); they may take the form of algorithms for diagnostic evaluation or treatment planning and implementation. The potential benefits of practice guidelines are clear, but they will be effective in improving the quality of care only to the extent that they are based on empirical evidence.

One very important structural characteristic of mental health and substance abuse treatment is the existence of large, relatively separate, publicly funded systems of care. The existence of dual systems of care provides opportunities for cost shifting, adverse selection, and a variety of other problems because the systems are managed separately and with differing objectives. Similarly, reduced access to certain kinds of care via management procedures may shift costs and other burdens of care from formal to informal providers—for example, family members and friends. Shorter hospital stays, for example, may shift part of the burden of stabilization and maintaining medication adherence from the hospital team to the patient's family and friends in the posthospitalization period.

Process. The process domain comprises a variety of elements in the interactions between the clinician and the patient or client, including both the clinician-client relationship and the clinician's technical skills (for example, diagnostic assessment, treatment planning, and delivery). The relationship between provider and client—sometimes referred to as the *therapeutic alliance*—has historically been a prominent element in psychiatric treatment. Changes introduced by managed care in the ways that providers can interact with their patients may change the relationship and thereby influence quality of care. Additionally, the relationship between process and outcome may be moderated by certain patient characteristics (for example, diagnosis), such that a specific process modification may change outcomes for some types of patients but not for others.

One critical process issue in managed behavioral health care involves the concept of appropriate care. Factors to be considered in assessing appropriateness include the patient's symptomatology and life circumstances (that is, needs), the level of restrictiveness of proposed care (for example, inpatient versus outpatient), the nature of the specific care (for example, pharmacologic, psychosocial), and the intensity or amount of care (for example, length of stay, number of sessions). Although many issues of appropriateness involve conflicting values, the debate over appropriateness is best conducted in the context of empirical evidence about the relationship of process to outcome.

Outcomes. For some, the bottom line with respect to quality of care is outcomes. It remains the case, however, that a good outcome does not necessarily mean high-quality care. Donabedian (1980) defined outcome as "a change in the patient's current and future health status [symptoms and functioning] that can be attributed to antecedent health care" (p. 82). Although his definition has two parts—that is, a patient's status must change, and that change must be attributable to health care received—most of the attention to date has been on the first part. Salzer and colleagues (1997) emphasize that assessing outcomes requires both evidence of change in status at follow-up *and* a design that supports valid causal inference. Much contemporary research supports description of posttreatment status but not causal attribution. Development of a database that both documents status at follow-up and supports valid causal inference is an extremely important challenge for the field.

Evaluating Managed Mental Health Care. Wells, Astrakhan, Tischler, and Unutzer (1995) discussed several challenges for evaluating managed mental health care, which generalize to some extent to the substance abuse arena as well (a point to be discussed later in this chapter). These challenges include the limited empirical evidence available to guide management decisions in a new but rapidly evolving field; the proprietary, competitive, and dynamic environment of managed care; the limitations of the available sources of data; and various confidentiality issues involving employers, insurers, and patients.

They also offer several principles for developing a valid empirical database that can support decisions about how best to manage care. Given the state of the field, they point out, descriptive information is valuable, and all stakeholders should document and improve the quality of proprietary datasets and establish mechanisms by which to pool data for analysis to inform the field in general and managed care decisions in particular. Mechanisms to document changes in benefits or service delivery also need to be implemented, so that such changes can be taken into account in outcome analyses. Independent evaluators—that is, persons possessing the substantive and methodological expertise who have no vested interest in the analytic outcomes—need to use the data in ways that yield better decisions and that take account of the various interests and perspectives involved.

Quality Issues and QA/QI Approaches for Substance Abuse

In *Managing Managed Care: Quality Improvement in Behavioral Health,* the Institute of Medicine (1997) noted three unusual aspects of the systems of care for both mental health and substance abuse. One is the presence of a publicly funded system that serves as a safety net for those without insurance. Although the distinction between public and private substance abuse treatment programs is not as clear as it once was, with public programs serving those with private insurance and private programs receiving public dollars, parallel substance abuse treatment systems remain. The flow of public dollars through the system creates special challenges. Many substance abuse treatment programs rely on various streams of public dollars, each with its own eligibility requirements and constraints; this in turn leads to gaps in or duplication of services and difficulties in adhering to the range of requirements that each of the financial sources may impose.

A second challenge is that the majority of patients with substance abuse problems are not served by speciality substance abuse programs. Many who need substance abuse treatment remain unserved, making access to care a particular concern. As Regier and colleagues (1993) note, among those who do receive services, nearly equal numbers are seen by primary care providers as are treated by speciality substance abuse providers. This raises concerns about the quality and variability of care according to the sector in which patients are seen.

Within specialized substance abuse treatment programs, the typical scenario is that clients abuse multiple drugs including alcohol; in addition, many have other medical and psychiatric conditions that also demand attention. Thus treatment for many patients not only focuses on their abuse of alcohol or other drugs but also includes rehabilitative and support services such as employment counseling, housing assistance, legal services, and family services. The range of services provided by a substance abuse treatment program is determined both by the needs of those served and by the availability of categorical funding streams to support these services. The diversity of services provided greatly increases the complexity of ensuring the quality of care.

Substance abuse treatment services are provided in a range of settings, including hospital-based inpatient care, other residential settings, and outpatient care. The 1980s saw the rapid expansion of twenty-eight-day inpatient programs, often referred to as Minnesota Model programs or chemical dependency units, as substance abuse treatment was increasingly accepted as a reimbursable service by insurance companies. The 1990s, with their emphasis on cost containment, have seen a significant reduction in the use of hospital care, with inpatient stays limited to three to five days for detoxification and initial stabilization before transferring a patient to a less intensive setting. This, in turn, has given rise to intensive outpatient programs, structured day and evening programs that the client attends for four to eight hours per day. The vast majority of those treated in substance abuse programs are now served in these programs. This shift in program settings has prompted a significant change in practice norms.

Substance abuse treatment has a longstanding tradition of involvement with self-help groups; Alcoholics Anonymous is the forerunner for much of the current treatment system. Similarly, many early programs for those who abuse other drugs were started by ex-addicts. This tradition has resulted in many service providers themselves being in recovery. Substance abuse treatment thus differs from mental health—and health care in general—with a focus on the experiential background of providers. Substance abuse has not historically placed as much importance on the academic background of providers as have the health and mental health sectors, although this is changing.

Quality Assurance Efforts in Substance Abuse. QA efforts in substance abuse have drawn heavily on developments in health care, yet in many programs these efforts are not well developed. Accreditation, a major impetus for formalized QA/QI, is not as widely employed by substance abuse treatment programs as by health care facilities and programs. Likewise, many programs have a heavy reliance on the self-help tradition, which has typically not emphasized the types of QI activities seen in programs based on the medical model.

A second difference with substance abuse treatment is the significant focus on access to care as an indicator of the quality of the treatment system. The emphasis reflects the development of the treatment field; early programs (in the 1940s) were started by those in recovery after they experienced difficulties in gaining access to needed services. Even today service availability and access to care are major issues; less than one-third of those needing services receive them.

Finally, treatment outcomes have played a prominent role in how the quality of substance abuse treatment services is assessed. One reason for this emphasis is the ongoing need to demonstrate effectiveness to gain support for treatment. In addition, this field involves a wide array of interventions provided by a variety of practitioners in a range of settings, with none gaining prominence as the accepted treatment process for substance abusers. This diversity in treatment interventions and settings makes it difficult to assess whether the treatment process is appropriate, leading to a focus on outcomes.

An Illustrative Case Study. The Methadone Treatment Quality Assurance System (MTQAS) project, funded by the National Institute on Drug Abuse, emerged in response to concerns raised by the General Accounting Office (1990) about the variability in quality in providing methadone to those addicted to opiates. Treatment of heroin or opioid addiction through the use of methadone (or more recently LAAM [levo-alpha-acetyl-methadol]) is a special case of substance abuse care, because it involves treating patients addicted to one substance with another addictive agent, one that federal agencies consider a "controlled substance." The effectiveness of methadone treatment for many patients is unquestioned, but the therapy, whether used alone or in combination with psychosocial interventions, is provided in opioid treatment programs (OTPs) or clinics that are closely regulated and overseen by various federal agencies (including the Food and Drug Administration and the Drug Enforcement Administration) and state regulatory authorities. Approximately one-third of these programs nationwide are closely tied to hospitals. The remainder either are freestanding clinics or are embedded in a larger organization, typically a substance abuse treatment program that serves a wide array of substance abuse problems. For many, contemporary ideas of QA or QI as understood in the mainstream health care sector have not, until recently, significantly penetrated the OTP arena.

MTQAS is beginning to fill that gap. Approximately seventy OTPs located in seven states are currently participating in MTQAS as part of a feasibility assessment of an outcomes-based performance measurement system for OTPs. OTPs treat opioid addiction as a long-term condition with the expectation that patients will remain in care for months or even years. MTQAS uses seventeen in-treatment outcomes to measure a program's performance, including drug use (measured by self-reports and urine tests), injecting behavior, program retention, employment, criminal justice involvement, health functioning, health and mental health care utilization, and patient satisfaction.

Results of these standardized assessments are funneled through the state substance abuse office to Research Triangle Institute (RTI), which prepares a quarterly performance report for each participating OTP. RTI's report provides each program with information on its own performance and comparisons to other OTPs in the state where the program is located and to all programs involved with MTQAS. These comparisons include case-mix-adjusted performance to account for the characteristics of the populations served.

Lessons from the MTQAS Experience. OTPs can function as service programs while implementing a performance monitoring system using outcome measures. Their experience provides several important lessons. First, OTPs can use information on patient outcomes to assess how they are doing and improve services. One program, for example, changed its clinical practices after receiving a report that its outcomes were below average; another used the quarterly report as a self-evaluation tool to assess the impact of revisions in its treatment protocols. Second, some programs require additional assistance; for a sample of programs with outcomes below expectations, the federal Center for Substance Abuse Treatment will provide technical assistance to help bridge the gap between outcomes and necessary program action. Third, states understand the value of this activity: one state has made such outcome monitoring a contractual requirement for all programs receiving state funds, and two others are considering specific strategies to encourage or require OTPs to continue monitoring outcomes.

If these positive indications are borne out, the next step will be to expand this type of effort beyond OTPs to all types of substance abuse treatment programs. Many of the concepts tested as part of MTQAS—including clinician-based assessments for ongoing monitoring of patient outcomes, regular feedback reports to programs, case-mix adjustment, and the choice of outcomes—can be readily transferred to these other programs.

Challenges Ahead for Behavioral Health

Numerous practical issues remain for those who would advance the science and art of QA/QI in behavioral health. Some challenges relate to the difficulties of measurement in these often complicated patient populations, including the complexities of specifying processes of care or defining appropriate outcomes to measure; moreover, patients may be cared for in a greater variety of settings, some of which are not typically covered in traditional QA/QI programs. Splitting off behavioral health care, whether mental health services or substance abuse treatment, from the rest of health care poses special obstacles for a clear picture of access to and quality of care across the range of needed and appropriate services. This is especially the case if patients with multiple problems receive regular health care through one plan or setting, mental health services through a separate plan or provider, and substance abuse therapies through yet another provider. When this happens the synergies across health, mental health, and substance abuse services are lost or attenuated, and so are the insights that might be gained from broader-based QA/QI efforts.

Ensuring adequate care for patients with mental health or substance abuse problems is not, however, simply a matter of better assessment tools or more advanced QA/QI programs. Various complicating political or philosophical issues must be addressed. Providers (and patients, and the public at large) may disagree about whether a "medical model" or a "medical and social model" is the preferable approach, and the resulting principles around which treatment programs are organized may have a significant impact on what would be regarded as substandard, acceptable, or superior care.

In concluding, we emphasize the need for more systematic development and use of valid information on structural characteristics of providers and on the processes and outcomes of care for patients with psychiatric and substance abuse disorders. This will be the vehicle through which the systems that provide care, whether integrated across primary and specialty settings or rendered in managed behavioral health care programs, can be established on the basis of empirical evidence gathered under designs that support valid causal inference, rather than opinion and conjecture, and can then be held to account for high-quality care for all patients.

References

Berwick, D. "Continuous Improvement as an Ideal in Health Care." *New England Journal of Medicine*, 1989, *320*, 53–56.

Chassin, M. R. "Assessing Strategies for Quality Improvement." *Health Affairs*, 1997, *16*, 151–161.

Donabedian, A. "Evaluating the Quality of Medical Care." *Milbank Memorial Fund Quarterly*, July 1966, *44* (Part 2), 166–203.

Donabedian, A. *Explorations in Quality Assessment and Monitoring: The Definition of Quality and Approaches to Its Assessment.* Vol. 1. Ann Arbor, Mich.: Health Administration Press, 1980.

General Accounting Office. *Methadone Maintenance: Some Treatment Programs Are Not Effective; Greater Federal Oversight Needed.* GAO/HRD–90–104. Washington, D.C.: U.S. General Accounting Office, 1990.

Institute of Medicine. *Medicare: A Strategy for Quality Assurance.* (K. N. Lohr, ed.). Washington, D.C.: National Academy Press, 1990.

Institute of Medicine. *Guidelines for Clinical Practice: From Development to Use.* (M. J. Field and K. N. Lohr, eds.). Washington, D.C.: National Academy Press, 1992.

Institute of Medicine. *Managing Managed Care: Quality Improvement in Behavioral Health.* (E. Edmunds, R. Frank, M. Hogan, D. McCarty, R. Robinson-Beale, and C. Weisner, eds.). Washington, D.C.: National Academy Press, 1997.

Miller, R. H., and Luft, H. S. "Does Managed Care Lead to Better or Worse Quality of Care?" *Health Affairs,* 1997, *16,* 7–25.

Palmer, R. H., and Lawthers, A. *CONQUEST 1.1: A Computerized Needs-Oriented Quality Measurement Evaluation System.* Rockville, Md.: Agency for Health Care Policy and Research, Apr. 1997.

Regier, D., Narrow, W., Rae, D., Manderscheid, R., Locke, B., and Goodwin, F. "The De Facto US Mental and Addictive Disorders Service System: Epidemiologic Catchment Area Prospective 1–Year Prevalence Rates of Disorders and Services." *Archives of General Psychiatry,* 1993, *50,* 85–94.

Salzer, M., Nixon, C., Schut, L., Karver, M., and Bickman, L. "Validating Quality Indicators: Quality as Relationship Between Structure, Process, and Outcome," *Evaluation Review,* 1997, *21,* 292–309.

Wells, K. B., Astrakhan, B. M., Tischler, G. L., and Unutzer, J. "Issues and Approaches in Evaluating Managed Mental Health Care." *Milbank Quarterly,* 1995, *73,* 57–75.

KATHLEEN N. LOHR *is director of the health services and policy research program in the Health and Social Policy Division of Research Triangle Institute, North Carolina.*

WILLIAM E. SCHLENGER *is director of the mental and behavioral health research program in the Health and Social Policy Division of Research Triangle Institute, North Carolina.*

J. WILLIAM LUCKEY *is director of the substance abuse treatment research program in the Health and Social Policy Division of Research Triangle Institute, North Carolina.*

The first nationwide survey on managed care's impact shows widespread concern among consumers with severe mental illnesses and their families.

Consumer and Family Views of Managed Care

Laura Lee Hall, Richard Beinecke

Fifteen states require that people with severe and persistent mental illnesses be enrolled in managed care programs in the public mental health system (Hall, Edgar, and Flynn, 1997). With passage of the Balanced Budget Act of 1997 and its easing of requirements for states to implement Medicaid managed care programs, undoubtedly many more states will quickly follow suit. Despite this rapid shift of a population facing severe and chronic disability into managed care and general concerns about risk-based financing approaches as applied to people with serious disabilities, little is known about consumer and family perceptions and experiences of managed care (Frank, Koyanagi, and McGuire, 1997). This chapter reports highlights of the results of what is, to the authors' knowledge, the first nationwide assessment of the views of managed care held by consumers with severe mental illnesses and their family members, and of their experiences with it. The results show that most respondents were not yet enrolled in managed care. While reflecting some positive experiences and hopes, the data strongly point to limited knowledge about managed care and deep concerns about this delivery system approach for people with ongoing and serious illnesses.

Survey Methodology

This survey was distributed to members of the National Alliance for the Mentally Ill (NAMI), a nationwide grassroots organization with 168,000 members. A six-

Note: Support for this research was provided, in part, by the Center for Mental Health Services in the Substance Abuse and Mental Health Services Administration, Public Health Services, U.S. Department of Health and Human Services.

teen-item questionnaire addressing characteristics of the respondents, sources of treatment and services, access to and quality of those services, and specific views and experiences of managed care was mailed to 1,200 NAMI members in April 1996. Specifically, at least 20 NAMI members from each state were randomly selected from the membership database. There were 373 responses, representing a 31.3 percent response rate. In addition, an abridged version of the survey was published in NAMI's publication *The Advocate,* which goes to the entire NAMI membership. An additional 438 members responded to *The Advocate* survey.

Responses were received from NAMI members in every single state and the District of Columbia. Eighty-two percent of the respondents were family members of individuals with a severe mental illness. Their response to the questionnaire was in reference to their ill family member. Eighteen percent of the responses came directly from individuals with a severe mental illness—primary consumers—answering the questions based on their own experiences in and perceptions of managed care.

Characteristics of Survey Respondents

Respondents to NAMI's survey represent individuals with severe mental illnesses that have persisted for some time. While the age of respondents varied, on average family member respondents were fifty and consumers forty years of age.

Schizophrenia was, by far, the most common diagnosis, accounting for 72 percent of clients. Diagnoses of bipolar illness and schizoaffective disorder were the second and third most common diagnoses, representing 14 percent and 9 percent respectively. It should be noted that there were some significant differences in the diagnoses reported by family members about primary consumers and reflected in primary consumer reports. Seventy-five percent of family members but only 38 percent of consumers indicated a primary diagnosis of schizophrenia. Only 12 percent of family members but 35 percent of consumer respondents identified a primary diagnosis of bipolar disorder. And while only 1 percent of family members indicated major depression as a primary diagnosis, 15 percent of the consumer respondents listed this as the primary illness.

Answers to the questions concerning service use also reflect a population facing serious illness. Thirty-one percent reported hospitalization in the past year for the primary mental illness diagnosis. More than three-quarters—76 percent—reported access to outpatient services during the past year. Ninety percent reported current use of medication. And nearly one-third reported additional problems with substance abuse or physical illness.

Source of Services

Clients had multiple funding sources for the treatment of mental illness. Half were enrolled in Medicaid or Medicare. A quarter received funding from the state or locality. A quarter also used private insurance to pay for treatment of their brain disorder while an additional 13 percent used services paid for out of their own pockets.

Nearly one-quarter—22 percent—of NAMI consumers received treatment for their severe mental illness in a managed care organization. This includes those enrolled in an HMO (13 percent of consumers, the majority of whom had private health insurance) and those enrolled in a managed behavioral health care organization or carve-out (9 percent of consumers, most of whom were enrolled in Medicaid programs). Over half (53 percent) were not enrolled in a managed care organization. Nineteen percent stated that services were received through some other type of organization, examples of which include community mental health centers, county mental health programs, and state hospitals. Reported rates of managed care enrollment were similar among family members and consumer respondents. Sixty-six respondents listed a managed care organization from which they were receiving care, representing forty-six different organizations.

Some confusion about health plan coverage was also evident. Organizations listed as "other" could be managed care organizations or not (for example, community mental health centers or county programs). Some respondents listed specific HMOs under "other." Also, 6 percent each of the responding family members and consumers did not know their enrollment status in managed care organizations. So even NAMI members, who are generally quite informed as consumers of health care, have uncertainties concerning their relationship to managed care programs.

Covered Services

Respondents reported significant limitations on the kinds of treatments and services covered by their current plan or program. In general, more traditional aspects of medical care enjoyed greater coverage. It is striking to note, however, that in some systems of care, crisis services (10 percent), intensive case management (22 percent), and even medication (10 percent) and doctor's visits (6 percent) are not covered at all. It is also of note that outside of hospitalization, medications, and outpatient visits, 22 percent to 50 percent of the respondents did not know about the coverage of other types of interventions.

While coverage generally did not vary greatly between those respondents enrolled in managed care versus those who were not, when it did, managed care almost always provided better coverage. Specifically, residential care, crisis services, home care, office visits, family psychoeducation and support, and intensive case management were more likely to be covered under managed care. The exception is substance abuse services, which were less likely to be covered under managed care. These data suggest that, at least in terms of coverage, consumers and family members perceive that managed care organizations provide for a richer palette of non–hospital-based care.

Access

Approximately 25 percent of all respondents reported *substantial* problems accessing care. Clearly, even for this group of individuals—who are generally skilled at using services—access is still frequently a major problem. Consumer respondents reported even more problems, especially in terms of getting timely services, accessing desired providers, or having to pay too much out of pocket.

In nearly every instance, as Table 8.1 shows, access problems were reported much more frequently by respondents enrolled in managed care organizations than by those who were not. For example, while 16 percent of respondents not enrolled in a managed care organization reported substantial problems getting a provider knowledgeable about severe mental illnesses, 29 percent of respondents in a managed care organization indicated this access problem. Similarly, while 18 percent of respondents not enrolled in a managed care organization reported substantial problems getting admitted to a hospital, 32 percent of the respondents enrolled in managed care reported such difficulties.

Quality of Care

The survey asked respondents to rate the quality of various services received in their current health care plan. Overall, the percentage of individuals who rated quality "good" is low. In only two areas—medications and office visits—did more than 50 percent of the NAMI survey respondents rate care as "good." Most other types of services received much poorer ratings. Psychosocial reha-

Table 8.1 Reported Access Problems

Have you or your family member had any substantial problems with any of the following access issues in your current health plan?	Respondents not enrolled in managed care (percent)	Respondents enrolled in managed care (percent)
Getting timely services?	23	42
Getting a provider knowledgeable about severe mental illnesses?	16	30
Getting admitted to a hospital?	18	32
Getting a culturally/linguistically approriate provider?	6	5
Knowing how to access treatment and services?	20	40
Getting desired provider?	19	31
Having to pay too much out of pocket for services?	19	37
Getting proper dose and type of medication?	22	36
Getting a provider in reasonably close geographic proximity?	12	16

bilitation services, respite care, and substance abuse services were rated particularly low.

Comparison of the rated quality of services in managed care versus non–managed care environments is not straightforward, as there was a mixture of views about the quality of care in each of the settings and some variation in service use. So, for example, many respondents not enrolled in managed care viewed services as "good" but many also viewed services as "poor." However, when services had been used, greater percentages of respondents not enrolled in managed care ranked quality to be "good" compared to respondents in managed care. It is noteworthy that a significant number of enrollees in HMOs—73 percent—rated primary health care services as good, compared to those not in managed care at all (45 percent) and those enrolled in behavioral carve-outs (39 percent).

Complaints, Appeals, and Grievances

The next series of survey questions focused on appeal and grievance processes. Specifically, we asked NAMI survey respondents if they knew how to file a complaint, grievance, or appeal; if they have ever filed one; and if so, how it was resolved.

Once again, lack of knowledge was a dominant trend. More than half the respondents—55 percent—reported that they do not know how to file such claims, whether they were in managed care or not. Of the respondents who knew how to file a complaint, grievance, or appeal, 18 percent indicated that they have filed one, again with similar results from consumers and family members. It is interesting to note that respondents enrolled in behavioral carve-outs were more likely to have filed a complaint, grievance, or appeal—26 percent—than those not in managed care (15 percent) or enrolled in an HMO (18 percent).

So what happened when respondents filed a complaint, grievance, or appeal? For 29 percent of the respondents, the action was resolved reasonably promptly and in their favor. Resolution in their favor was also achieved for another 17 percent, but over a long time frame. For 26 percent, an unfavorable result was reported—and for 29 percent there never was any resolution. These results varied among consumer and family member respondents: many more consumers reported that their efforts to seek redress went unresolved—48 percent versus 25 percent.

Different types of health plans produced different patterns of complaint, grievance, and treatment appeal results. Most notably, the behavioral managed health care organizations had the highest rates of unresolved entreaties—42 percent of NAMI survey respondents who complained, versus 29 percent of both those enrolled in HMOs and those not enrolled in managed care at all.

Hopes and Concerns for Managed Care

The final sections of the survey asked NAMI members to indicate their concerns and hopes for managed care by checking off a list of potential concerns and benefits. Respondents were also given the opportunity to provide additional comments. Figure 8.1 summarizes the responses to the question, "What do you feel are the major concerns as well as promises of managed care's application to people with severe mental illnesses?" With one exception (confidentiality) over 50 percent of the respondents expressed concern about all the potential problems listed in the NAMI survey. The greatest concerns focused on the availability of and access to needed treatment. Only one-quarter of the survey respondents saw any benefits in managed care.

Consumers and family members generally had similar concerns about managed care, although consumers voiced much greater concern about losing the confidentiality of their medical records—61 percent versus 39 percent of the family member respondents.

Experience in managed care only served to increase concerns about access to mental illness treatment. Individuals enrolled in managed care organizations had greater concerns about the issues of treatment eligibility and denial of treatment than those not enrolled in managed care organizations. Fifty-one percent of managed care enrollees expressed concern about eligibility for treatment versus 37 percent of nonenrollees. Similarly, 74 percent of managed care enrollees expressed concern about treatment denial versus 67 percent of the nonenrollees. More than 80 percent of the respondents enrolled in carve-out organizations were especially concerned about the availability of treatment and treatment denial. Only two potential benefits of managed care were viewed differently by managed care enrollees versus those who were not. Twenty-four percent of the nonenrollees believed unnecessary hospitalization would be decreased, versus 33 percent of the managed care enrollees. Seventeen percent of the nonenrollees believed it would be easier to obtain medical (non–mental health) treatment as compared with 29 percent of enrollees.

Replies to the open-ended question confirmed many of the item responses:

- Many respondents do not know much about managed care. Many are not in managed care programs or are in states where such programs are just being introduced.
- NAMI members described many problems with their existing non–managed care services. Mental health services, whether managed or not, pose many problems for persons and families confronting severe mental illnesses.
- NAMI members have had positive experiences with managed care. Some persons reported that additional services such as clubhouses have been added by managed care programs. Some said that local staff were hired by managed care groups, and that staff seemed energized to do things in a new way. Under HMOs, some reported, there was a closer linkage between medical and mental health care.
- Others said that there had been no changes, either positive or negative, under managed care.

Figure 8.1 Reported Perceptions of Benefit and Risk

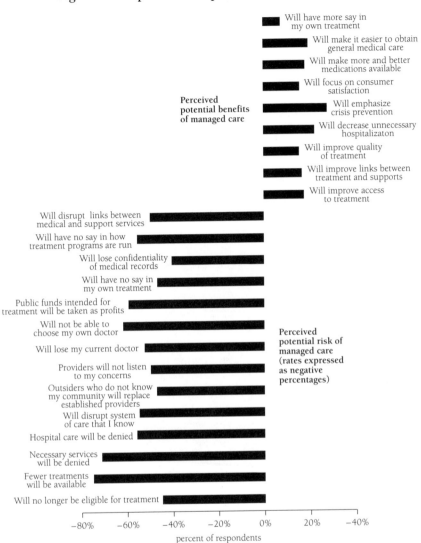

Nonetheless, most NAMI members expressed concerns about managed care based on their direct experience of managed care or what they have heard. In general, their concerns focus on too-shortened hospital stays, lack of support services, rigid procedures, and general reductions in access to care.

Conclusions

This survey was addressed to NAMI members who were largely self-selected, which limits broad generalizations. Nonetheless, several themes suggest trends and concerns that warrant further research and resonate with the impression of the authors and many others considering managed care's impact.

The survey respondents gave voice to the observation that managed care expands benefits even as it more stringently restricts access to services. Added to these observations is the view that many support services, part and parcel of a truly comprehensive system of care, continue to be missing in managed care. Frank and his associates (1997) have noted that gains in parity are realized by managed care's ability to contain cost; they caution that, by different means, managed care's restrictions on service may pose similar dangers to limited benefit structures in terms of access to needed treatment and services. A broadened benefit definition is not necessarily an advantage if access is prohibitively restrictive. A longer list of benefits does not equal a truly comprehensive system of care for people with chronic and severely disabling mental illnesses.

NAMI members do not proclaim existing non–managed care service systems to be of high quality. But according to those surveyed managed care does not appear to enhance the quality of treatments and supports. With extensive scientific documentation of treatments and services that are effective for treating severe mental illnesses, poor quality—whether in managed care or outside it—should be unacceptable.

Some types of managed care seem to have significantly improved a persistent problem for persons with serious mental illness—access to basic medical treatment for non–mental illness problems. Enrollees in HMOs, as opposed to behavioral carve-outs, reported improved access to general health care. Further efforts are needed to better integrate mental health care with good general health services.

Particularly disturbing results from this survey are the limits of knowledge about the health plan in which NAMI members are enrolled and their limited awareness of how to register complaints. In an era of so-called increased consumer choice and power, this lack of information at the very least gives the lie to the popular rhetoric. Consumers and family members seem to be poorly equipped to influence the increasingly complex systems.

Overall, NAMI members are generally skeptical about the shift to managed care. They see this system change as presenting new risks of limiting access to needed treatment and services, without substantially improving other aspects of the quality of care. Furthermore, the transition to managed care appears to increase the complexity and incomprehensibility of the system on which consumers with chronic illnesses and their families depend. These concerns raise basic issues about the value that capitation and managed care add to a too-frequently failing system.

References

Frank, R. G., Koyanagi, C., and McGuire, T. G. "The Politics and Economics of Mental Health 'Parity' Laws." *Health Affairs,* 1997, *16,* 108–119.

Hall, L. L., Edgar, E. R., and Flynn, L. M. *Stand and Deliver: Action Call to a Failing Industry. The NAMI Managed Care Report Card.* Arlington, Va.: National Alliance for the Mentally Ill, 1997.

LAURA LEE HALL is the deputy director of policy and research, National Alliance for the Mentally Ill.

RICHARD BEINECKE is an assistant professor in the Department of Public Management, Suffolk University.

Managed care contracting reflects the fundamental tensions that arise when organizations whose operations depend in large part on standardization and control sell their services to purchasers with more or less specific and often nonstandardized expectations.

Behavioral Health Contracting

Sara Rosenbaum

In a single generation the American health care system has evolved from a collection of small independent businesses to one in which large and midsized companies known as managed care organizations (MCOs) offer enrolled members specified health care for a preset fee. In 1996, about 75 percent of privately insured Americans, 12 percent of Medicare beneficiaries, and nearly 40 percent of Medicaid beneficiaries were enrolled in managed care. Some MCOs offer general services modeled on a major medical insurance plan, typically supplemented by preventive coverage. Others specialize in certain product lines such as mental health and addiction disorder treatment services (commonly known as behavioral health care).

Legal Background

MCOs merge health insurance and medical care practice into health care products, creating virtual health systems through a cascade of subcontracts. Participating providers, selected by MCOs and subject to their rules, share their financial and service-related risks. In turn, MCOs enter into complex contracts with their group purchasers that define the product they are expected to sell and the terms by which they will be paid. Understanding the contracts that bind the system together can help policymakers grasp the nature of the changes that are taking place.

Contracts are integral to the framework of the new health system, as the legal basis of health care moves from common law principles of professionalism and regulation to market principles and tools, of which contracts are the prime example. In a single generation, propelled by the deregulatory effects of ERISA and the application of antitrust principles to health care (Rosenblatt, Law, and Rosenbaum, 1997), the old legal foundation crumbled, a victim of rampant price increases (which threatened to make even basic health coverage unaffordable) and mounting evidence of widespread, costly, and inexplicable variations in health care practice. As federal and state policymakers now struggle with the task of building a new statutory framework for health care (Moran, 1997; Rosenblatt, Law, and Rosenbaum, 1997), contracts still dominate the legal landscape and will continue to do so in light of the relatively inconsequential effects of much of the (even widely heralded) legislation being written today (Kuttner, 1997).

The Meaning of Contracts. Voluntarily negotiated agreements between buyers and sellers on one hand, and sellers and suppliers on the other, form the legal basis on which the health system is organized. Contracts are the tools that formalize these voluntary arrangements and that—in the absence of publicly enacted laws—offer at least some semblance of legally enforceable expectations for system stakeholders. A contract creates legally binding and enforceable promises on those who enter into an agreement, and contract enforcement constitutes one of the principal means by which societal interests are advanced and protected in a market-oriented, deregulated economy.

Proponents of a market health system advocate for the use of contracts as a means of legally ordering the system (Havighurst, 1992); but the legal principles underlying contract interpretation and enforcement are markedly different from those underlying statutory and regulatory interpretation and enforcement. Where government is a party to a contract, the results of an enforcement effort can be quite different from the world of regulation. Learning to use contracts well thus constitutes a major task, both for government agencies used to the principles that accompany legislatively established standards and for private actors unfamiliar with the consequences of signing private agreements they may have neither read nor understood.

Contracts and Government Agencies. Contracts offer distinct advantages over legislatively created law. However, contract negotiation and enforcement also create new challenges for government buyers. Unlike legislation and rules, which are publicly created through a long, arduous process, contracts can be rapidly and privately negotiated, even in cases in which a buyer such as an employer or union owes fiduciary or trust obligations to the individuals on whose behalf a purchase is made. However, where government is a party, public procurement principles make the contracting process a much more open and regulated one, in light of the public accountability to which government purchasers are held. Thus, when a public agency buys managed care services on a competitive basis, the procurement process can be lengthy and difficult, thereby vitiating some of the advantages of contracting.

Government purchasers face other contract problems. Under the principles of statutory construction and administrative law that govern the interpretation of statutes and regulations, courts give great deference to government when asked to construe the meaning of an ambiguously worded law or regulation. Contract interpretation principles are completely different. Under principles of contract law, where a contract is vaguely worded, courts will give no special level of judicial deference to one party merely because it is the government. A government purchaser cannot, as with regulations, clarify a vague provision with subsequent unilateral pronouncements regarding the meaning of terms. Because a contract memorializes a private agreement as opposed to a publicly debated standard, the rule of *contra proferentem* (a contract is construed against the drafter) applies, since courts assume that the parties were capable of reaching a clear understanding as to the meaning of their agreement and that the duty lies with the drafter to memorialize it in an honest fashion. Thus government agencies—accustomed to both broad judicial deference and the ability to issue unilateral statements interpreting the meaning of statutes and rules—may find their powers diminished as their post hoc clarification capabilities in relation to legal ambiguities in the document virtually disappear.

Many stakeholders in addition to the prime buyers, unaccustomed to contract principles, may fail to appreciate the import of the agreements they sign. Thus, for example, physicians who enter into managed care agreements may find themselves bound by duties and exposed to financial risks that they did not appreciate at the time they entered into the arrangement. Moreover, in a world of oversupply, physicians may find that they are at such a market disadvantage when bargaining with a buyer (whether a managed care organization with a prime contract or a subsidiary organization selling a particular good or service) that even when they understand the implications of the agreement they are relatively powerless to negotiate its terms (Rosenbaum and others, 1997).

Studies of Behavioral Health Managed Care Contracts

In 1995 the Center for Health Policy Research of the George Washington University Medical Center undertook two special studies for the Substance Abuse and Mental Health Services Administration. The first study examined contracts between managed care organizations and community providers of mental illness and addiction disorder treatment and prevention services (Rosenbaum, Silver, and Wehr, 1997a). The second study explored master service agreements between state Medicaid agencies and managed care organizations furnishing behavioral health services (either as part of a comprehensive coverage package or on a carve-out basis) on either a partial- or full-risk basis (Rosenbaum, Silver, and Wehr, 1997a).

Contracts Between Managed Care Organizations and Community Providers. The provider contract study is a point-in-time, descriptive study. In approaching this study, researchers considered the assumptions that underlie managed care and built a review instrument used by the attorneys who conducted the study and designed to test how, and the extent to which, company contracts attempt to accommodate and implement MCO expectations.

Group buyers of managed care products have several major goals when they enter into managed care agreements. First, the buyer expects that the managed care organization either directly or through its subcontractors will provide or arrange for the provision of services covered under the contract. Second, an MCO anticipates that it will select a qualified and price-conscious network and will establish effective procedures to continuously measure and oversee the quality of care. Third, the MCO expects to be able to stay within its agreed-upon budget and oversee the consumption of resources by members.

Managed care organizations may employ health care providers to carry out their service duties. More commonly, however, MCOs build their health systems through contracts either with individual providers or increasingly with provider networks that themselves assume the same duties of care, cost containment, and control. Because the basic duties of managed care organizations are similar regardless of the particular nomenclature of the managed care arrangement, MCO contracts are highly similar across different classes of entities. Many MCOs use standard contracts and generally resist detailed negotiations with individual groups of providers given their need to execute many individual contracts.

In light of the glut of health care providers in many communities, managed care organizations enjoy a superior bargaining position and have therefore been able to incorporate several important leverage points into virtually all contracts reviewed. These leverage points are (1) the "at will" nature of the agreement, which allows the organization to terminate the contract at any time and without cause; (2) a duty of care to furnish services covered under the agreement to all members referred to the network provider; (3) retention of residual authority in the organization over the assignment of patients to providers, so that there is no guarantee that a provider will receive all the members who select it; (4) "evergreen" and unilateral modification rights that permit the contract to continue indefinitely and without changes in its payment or performance provisions while at the same time permitting the company to alter provisions at any time with simple notice; (5) virtually total discretion to establish practice standards and determine which items and services covered under the organization's master agreement with the buyer are necessary and appropriate for the provider to furnish; and (6) payment terms that permit the organization to shift financial risk for cost overruns to the provider without liability for supplemental payment for care and services that the provider is obligated to furnish. These elements were evident in contracts studied regardless of whether the managed care organization was a comprehensive service HMO, a carve-out company, the holder of the master agreement with the buyer or a managed care subcontractor (for example, a physician services network), for profit or not for profit, provider owned or publicly traded.

The contracts represent a reversal of common law and traditional statutory law principles in several respects. First, the contracts create a duty of care on the part of network providers to care for plan members assigned to them. Network providers no longer select their patients—managed care organizations do. Indeed, by reserving discretion to assign members and specifying that providers will care only for patients referred to them (particularly common in the behavioral health provider contracts because of the specialty nature of the service), managed care organizations retain control over patient flow as well as the discretion to divert a provider's patients to another provider (an especially important means of securing practice and payment concessions from network providers).

Organizational control over medical care decision making represents another contractual departure from the past. By merging medical care practice and payment into a single corporate entity, managed care in effect creates a corporate standard of care that is grounded in quantitative scientific data and that rejects professional judgment (Bovbjerg, 1975; Eddy, 1994). Physicians find themselves in the middle of this unresolved issue of what constitutes the appropriate standard of care, as they remain liable under standards of professionalism even as the corporations of which they are a part move to a new standard (Rosenblatt, Law, and Rosenbaum, 1997).

Managed care contracts also depart from prior arrangements in their elimination of physicians' traditional right to determine when, how much, and for what they will be paid. Care and payment provisions are part of the contract, as are risk-sharing arrangements. Indeed, even where a physician has carefully negotiated an agreement with reasonable payment arrangements, the unilateral modification provisions commonly found in these contracts permit the organization to alter payment rules on notice, and the "at will" aspect of the contracts permit the organization to terminate the agreements of providers that protest. While in recent years several courts and legislatures have begun to recognize certain due process rights for network providers (Rosenblatt, Law, and Rosenbaum, 1997), "at-will" termination and unilateral modification provisions are still the norm.

Contracts Between Managed Care Organizations and State Medicaid Agencies. The move to mandatory Medicaid managed care began in the early 1980s. It accelerated during the 1990s through the use of federal statutory demonstration authority (Rosenbaum and Darnell, 1997b). By 1996 nearly two in five Medicaid beneficiaries were enrolled in some form of managed care plan; two-thirds were members of organizations operating at full or financial risk (Kaiser Commission on the Future of Medicaid, 1997).

Background. The Balanced Budget Act of 1997 permits states to establish mandatory managed care arrangements for most beneficiaries as a state option and without having to seek demonstration authority (Congressional Research Service, 1997). State-option waiver programs may be instituted for both nondisabled children and disabled adults with mental illness and addiction disorders (Congressional Research Service, 1997; Rosenbaum and Darnell, 1997b). In recent years, states have indicated their desire to move the disabled population into managed care—with or without waivers (National Academy for State Health Policy, 1997).

Under federal law, states that elect to provide managed care must enter into written, legally enforceable agreements, and contracts must comply with certain minimum elements, including specification of coverage services, minimum access and quality standards, and provisions to curb fraud and abuse (Rosenbaum and Darnell, 1997a). However, states retain a high degree of discretion over the structure of their agreements, and developing these contracts is extremely difficult. Medicaid agencies purchase products on behalf of populations with significant health needs and with incomes too low to buy additional care out of their own pockets. Moreover, Medicaid agencies cannot afford to buy point-of-service products that offer greater latitude in beneficiary use of health services. Medicaid managed care products thus create health systems far closer to traditional prepaid health plans than today's point-of-service products (Rosenbaum, Silver, and Wehr, 1997b).

Other factors make Medicaid managed care purchasing challenging. The first and most conceptually difficult issue from a legal point of view relates to the policy chasm that separates Medicaid coverage from insurance coverage. Federal Medicaid law and state Medicaid plans cover far more classes of services than are included in a typical insurance contract, managed care or otherwise. Medicaid covers not only the acute and primary care services customarily found in private insurance agreements but also long-term ambulatory and inpatient care for chronically and seriously mentally and physically ill persons.

Furthermore, the depth of Medicaid coverage for any particular class of service is significantly greater than under private insurance principles (Rosenbaum and others, 1997). Traditional insurance principles limit coverage to services that are calculated to restore "normal functioning" in persons suffering from "illnesses and injuries"—whereas Medicaid pays for services for persons who suffer from "conditions" such as developmental disabilities, illnesses, and injuries from which they will not recover. For this reason, many claims that are rejected by private insurers may nonetheless be covered by Medicaid, even when the two sources of third-party financing appear to be nominally the same (Rosenblatt, Law, and Rosenbaum, 1997).

Because Medicaid beneficiaries enrolled in managed care do not lose their Medicaid entitlement, states remain directly liable for all covered noncontract services. The issue is of great consequence for persons with serious mental illness or addiction disorders who may "fall through the cracks" as the state agency and the managed care organization dispute coverage liability. Moreover, in a typical managed care contract, coverage liability and care responsibility are integrated. Thus, MCOs that do not consider themselves liable for coverage would not arrange for the care in question. Drafting contract specifications that accurately delineate the respective duties of MCOs and state agencies is exceedingly difficult (Rosenbaum, Silver, and Wehr, 1997b).

Furthermore, MCOs also may not be accustomed to the needs of Medicaid beneficiaries. Some MCOs specialize in Medicaid care. Many others sell products to an employed population with primary and short-term acute care needs and are not equipped in terms of network or structure to care for the chronically ill poor. Finally, Medicaid managed care membership is contingent on Medicaid coverage; thus, enrollment periods can be very short, because Medicaid eligibility itself may last for only short time periods (about nine months) (National Committee for Quality Assurance, 1997). Short enrollment periods make adapting to managed care more difficult and potentially encourage underservice.

Study Results. In 1995 the George Washington University Center for Health Policy Research undertook a nationwide study of Medicaid managed care contracts. The project yielded rich findings regarding Medicaid managed care contracts. The study identified a series of principal domains addressed by all contracts: eligibility and enrollment; coverage; service delivery and access; public health and social service agency relationships; quality assurance, data, and reporting; business terms and relationships; and payment. The principal findings of the study underscored the practical and conceptual challenges that arise when converting Medicaid from a third-party payer to a purchaser of insurance.

With very limited exceptions, states open enrollment to persons with mental illness and addiction disorders (indeed, the Americans with Disabilities Act and the Rehabilitation Act of 1973 would prohibit states from arbitrarily denying enrollment based on disability). Therefore, in most states, any participating managed care organization could expect to have members with these conditions regardless of its obligation to provide services for mental illness and addiction.

Moreover, the study found that virtually all states included in their contracts fewer services for persons with mental or addiction disorders than those covered under the state plan, thereby increasing the likelihood of dual coverage. States varied widely in the classes and level of mental illness and addiction care that contractors were expected to provide. Moreover, about half of all contracts were silent on the standard to be applied, thereby resulting in a default to the industry standard. At least one contract expressly contained an "evidence-based" medical necessity standard that would permit a plan to exclude professional judgment from the evidence that it would consider in making coverage and care determinations (Rosenbaum, Silver, and Wehr, 1997b).

The study also revealed enrollment challenges, which are great in mandatory systems that rely on default enrollment for individuals who fail to select a plan. No contracts required plans to have special capabilities for default-enrolled beneficiaries with mental or addiction-related illnesses and disorders, and most contracts other than the special behavioral carve-out arrangements permitted companies to seek the disenrollment of members considered by the company to be "disruptive." Most contracts allowed plans virtually total discretion to build their networks and contained few access specifications designed to promote use of care among persons with mental illness or addiction disorders. Only two agreements required the use of specified clinical practice guidelines and outcome measures. Finally, the study found that few states had begun to address the complex issues that can arise as managed care companies increasingly enroll individuals who are under the care of multiple treatment and service systems, each of which operates in accordance with specific coverage and care rules, and most of which have come to depend heavily on Medicaid to finance the health and medical component of their programs.

Conclusion

As policymakers struggle to understand the dynamics of the new health system and to develop a measured approach to its regulation, it is important to understand the contracts that bind the system together. The two layers of contracts described in this chapter reveal a fundamental tension within managed care. On one hand, the managed care industry—like any large and highly complex enterprise—depends on standardization, stability, and control over its component parts. This dependence is underscored in the provider contracts. These contracts reflect MCOs' need to control their networks both financially and professionally in order to meet their buyers' expectations. On the other hand, purchasers expect that managed care products will be tailored to their needs and may wish to avoid standardization.

This tension is particularly evident in the case of Medicaid, because of the unique aspects of the underlying law and the special needs of many beneficiaries. Medicaid agencies need singular managed care products in certain respects; most have made a substantial effort to negotiate these special considerations into their contracts. Unfortunately, the process of contract development and negotiation is difficult and resources are severely constrained. As a result, many agencies may find that as they move from government payer to insurance purchaser, they have traded in one set of problems for a new and potentially larger set of challenges. It is likely, however, that federal and state policymakers will increasingly fashion minimum standards for the new health system, particularly as long as quality-of-care measurement remains relatively crude and consumer uneasiness with the effects of managed care on access and quality persists.

References

Bovbjerg, R. "The Medical Malpractice Standard of Care: HMOs and Customary Practice." *Duke Law Journal,* 1975, pp. 1375–1407.

Congressional Research Service. *An Analysis of the Medicare Provisions of the Balanced Budget Act of 1997.* Washington D.C.: Congressional Research Service, Aug. 1997.

Eddy, D. "Rationing Resources While Improving Quality: How to Get More for Less." *Journal of the American Medical Association,* 1994, 272, 817–827.

Havighurst, C. "Prospective Self-Denial: Can Consumers Contract Today to Accept Health Care Rationing Tomorrow?" *University of Pennsylvania Law Review,* 1992, 140, 1755.

Kuttner, R. "The Kassebaum-Kennedy Bill: The Limits of Incrementalism." *New England Journal of Medicine,* 1997, 330, 64–67.

Moran, D. "Regulating Managed Care: An Impulse in Search of a Theory?" *Health Affairs,* 1997, 16, 7–21.

National Academy for State Health Policy. *Medicaid Managed Care: Guide for the States.* (3rd ed.) Portland, Maine: National Academy for State Health Policy, 1997.

National Committee for Quality Assurance. *Medicaid HEDIS.* Washington D.C.: National Committee for Quality Assurance, 1997.

Rosenbaum, S., and Darnell, J. *A Comparison of the Medicaid Provisions in the Balanced Budget Act of 1997 (P. L. 103–33) with Prior Law.* Washington, D.C.: Kaiser Commission on the Future of Medicaid, 1997a.

Rosenbaum, S., and Darnell, J. *Statewide Medicaid Managed Care Demonstrations Under Section 1115 of the Social Security Act: A Review of the Waiver Applications, Letters of Approval and Special Terms and Conditions.* Washington, D.C.: Kaiser Commission on the Future of Medicaid, 1997b.

Rosenbaum, S., Shin, P., Smith, B., Wehr, E., Borzi, P., Zakhiem, M., Shaw, K., and Silver, K. *Negotiating the New Health System: A Nationwide Study of Medicaid Managed Care Contracts.* Washington, D.C.: George Washington University Medical Center, 1997.

Rosenbaum, S., Silver, K., and Wehr, E. *An Evaluation of Contracts Between Managed Care Organizations and Community Mental Health and Substance Abuse Treatment and Prevention Agencies.* Rockville, Md.: Substance Abuse and Mental Health Services Administration, 1997a.

Rosenbaum, S., Silver, K., and Wehr, E. *An Evaluation of Contracts Between State Medicaid Agencies and Managed Care Organizations for the Prevention and Treatment of Mental Illness and Substance Abuse Disorders.* Rockville, Md.: Substance Abuse and Mental Health Services Administration, 1997b.

Rosenblatt, R., Law, S., and Rosenbaum, S. *Law and the American Health Care System.* Old Westbury, N.Y.: Foundation Press, 1997.

SARA ROSENBAUM *is professor of health services management and policy at The George Washington University School of Public Health and Health Services, professor of health care sciences at The George Washington University Medical School, and director of the Center for Health Policy Research, The George Washington University Medical Center.*

PART THREE

Case Studies

Capitation reduced Medicaid costs but had limited effects on most measures of process and outcome. Clients under capitation with the poorest mental health at baseline performed more poorly over time on some measures.

The Effect of the Utah Prepaid Mental Health Plan on Structure, Process, and Outcomes of Care

Nicole Lurie, Jon B. Christianson, Donald Z. Gray, Willard G. Manning Jr., Michael K. Popkin

Many states are implementing carve-out approaches to mental health under Medicaid in which responsibility for providing care is assumed by an entity under contract in return for a capitated payment (Essock and Goldman, 1995; Koyanagi, 1996). Under most such arrangements, either a single entity contracts with the state to serve all Medicaid beneficiaries (for example, Leadholm and Kerzner, 1993; Micali and Nardini, 1996) or the state contracts with local, community-based mental health providers to serve Medicaid beneficiaries in their catchment areas (for example, Christianson, Gray, Kihlstrom, and Speckman, 1995; Babigian, Mitchell, Marshall, and Reed, 1992). Irrespective of the specifics of the managed care arrangement, most studies have concluded that state Medicaid programs have saved money, at least in the short term and for subgroups of beneficiaries, and that this has been accomplished primarily through reduced hospital use (Dwyer, Mitchell, Cole, and Reed, 1995; Christianson, Manning, and others, 1995; Stoner and others, 1997; Callahan and

Note: We acknowledge the support for this research that was provided by the National Institute for Mental Health and the Health Care Financing Administration, Department of Health and Human Services. We are grateful for the assistance provided by our research collaborators, Tamara Stoner, Chuan-Fen Liu, Jeffrey Harman, David Wyant, Sally Marriott, Allan Callies, Lucille Kihlstrom, and Barbara Coleman; the Health Care Financing Division, Department of Health, State of Utah; the community mental health centers in Utah; the data abstractors and interviewers who worked on the project; and especially the survey respondents.

others, 1995; Reed, Hennessy, Mitchell, and Babigian, 1994). Published evaluations regarding the effects of Medicaid managed care arrangements on the process and outcomes of care have been less conclusive. In this chapter, we examine these effects in the context of the Medicaid carve-out arrangement implemented by the State of Utah—the Utah Prepaid Mental Health Plan (UPMHP).

Background

The UPMHP began in July 1991, with three of Utah's eleven community mental health centers (CMHCs) participating in the contracts as providers. (For a description of the development and early operations of the UPMHP, see Christianson, Gray, Kihlstrom, and Speckman, 1995; "Utah Prepaid Mental Health Plan," 1996; Dangerfield and Betit, 1993). The contractors agreed to provide mental health services (excluding medications, substance abuse treatment, or state hospital stays) to all Medicaid beneficiaries residing in their catchment areas in return for a capitated payment. During the first two and a half years, the contractors were effectively at risk for inpatient but not outpatient care. Subsequently, the CMHCs in the plan were at risk for both.

The CMHCs in the plan reduced the use of inpatient care by beneficiaries in their catchment areas in comparison to other CMHCs (Christianson, Manning, and others, 1995; Stoner and others, 1997). The average use of outpatient services was not affected, with outpatient expenditures and visits trending upward in the catchment areas of CMHCs throughout the state (Stoner and others, 1997). Overall, however, the analysis suggests that the UPMHP reduced spending by the Medicaid program in Utah. What can be said about the program's impact on the structure, process, or outcomes of care?

Conceptual Framework

McGlynn and others (1988) argue that it is important to adopt as an evaluative framework—"an integrative approach that simultaneously examines the outcomes, the processes associated with producing those outcomes, and the structural context in which the process was delivered" (p. 159). In this framework, *outcomes* encompass such matters as clinical symptoms, functioning, mortality, quality of life, and societal costs. *Process of care* includes the diagnostic evaluation and the treatment approach. *Structure* includes the configuration of the mental health system, organizational and provider characteristics, method of payment, and patient characteristics.

Several factors complicate the application of this framework to Medicaid managed mental health care initiatives. For example, in assessing either process of care or its outcomes, there are few widely accepted "gold standards" against which to compare observed practices or their end results. Also, Medicaid beneficiaries have varying periods of eligibility and only a small subset receive mental health services in any given time period (Wright and Buck, 1991). Thus evaluation strategies that rely on a straight random sample of Medicaid beneficiaries to assess process or outcome of care would be impractical because very large sample sizes would be necessary in order to detect differences. However, a sampling frame identified after the fact based on service use could give misleading results. Therefore, studies that track mental health outcomes or processes of care over time must focus on a predetermined subset of Medicaid beneficiaries at high risk for use of mental health services.

Our evaluation focused on Medicaid beneficiaries with schizophrenia for several reasons. First, treatment interventions can favorably influence the course of the disease. Second, the prevalence is sufficient to permit a beneficiary-level analysis. Third, the costs of both treating and not treating the disease are high; beneficiaries with schizophrenia are frequent users of mental health services and, compared to many other persons with mental health diagnoses, are at relatively high risk of hospitalization. Fourth, claims algorithms have been developed and validated, so beneficiaries can be identified prospectively (Lurie, Moscovice, Popkin, and Dysken, 1992). However, schizophrenia is not always easy to diagnose and there is a wide range in the severity of illness (McGlynn and others, 1988).

The selection of this population as an evaluation focus is also appealing because of its potential to contribute to the national policy debate about extending capitation payment models to vulnerable populations. In particular, some policy analysts have expressed concern that severely mentally ill people may not secure necessary treatment under capitated arrangements (Schlesinger and Mechanic, 1993; Schlesinger, 1986). People with schizophrenia are certainly among the most vulnerable of Medicaid beneficiaries, and any effects of possible undertreatment arguably would be observable in this group.

We applied the framework proposed by McGlynn and colleagues to our evaluation of the UPMHP. We compared a wide range of measures for beneficiaries who received care from UPMHP providers and beneficiaries who received care from providers in areas of the state not covered by the UPMHP. While the comparison group does not provide a "gold standard," it does provide a relevant context for assessing changes in the UPMHP sites over time. We documented structure-related measures prior to the initiation of the UPMHP and for the first three years of the UPMHP's operations at both UPMHP and non-UPMHP sites, using published information on CMHC staffing and encounters, financial statements supplied by the CMHCs, and site visits to the CMHCs. Since the CMHC is the unit of analysis for these comparisons and there are only eleven CMHCs in Utah, the comparisons are necessarily qualitative in nature.

For the examination of process and outcomes, we considered the Medicaid beneficiary as the unit of analysis. We based our outcomes analysis on survey data collected at five points in time over a three-and-a-half-year period from Medicaid beneficiaries who were diagnosed with schizophrenia at the time the UPMHP was initiated. We measured mental health status and functioning at baseline so that we could use it to control for baseline severity in our statistical analysis and to analyze subgroups of patients defined by baseline disease severity. To address process, we used survey responses, supplemented with medical records data for a subsample of surveyed beneficiaries for the year prior to the UPMHP and the first three years of the UPMHP.

Measures of Structure

Financial Health of the CMHCs. The financial health of the CMHCs is a potentially important influence on process of care; if it deteriorates, pressures to limit treatment—resulting in worse patient outcomes—could occur. We found relatively few differences in standard financial measures between CMHCs that didn't already exist prior to the UPMHP. With or without UPMHP contracts, the CMHCs had strong financial growth, allowing for increases in fixed assets and cash reserves. We found no evidence that the UPMHP created financial conditions for CMHCs that potentially threatened patient care (Wyant, Christianson, and Coleman, 1997).

Programs and Staffing. At the operational level, CMHCs with UPMHP contracts experienced increases in the number of patients they served. They expanded children's programs, day treatment programs, and case management. Most important, the UPMHP did not precipitate an organizational crisis in any of these CMHCs, nor did it result in extensive organizational expansion. The CMHCs in this group appeared to adjust their programs and staffing over time in reasonable ways in response to their contractual responsibilities to their Medicaid beneficiaries.

Quality Assurance. Quality assurance processes and policies employed by the CMHCs varied considerably, but this variation appeared unrelated to participation in the UPMHP.

Summary. Using a variety of structural measures, we found no indication that CMHCs with UPMHP contracts were adversely affected. They remained financially healthy, implemented new programs that expanded outpatient care resources available for their patients, and revised and improved their quality assurance policies and activities.

Measures of Process

We documented the process of care for Medicaid beneficiaries with schizophrenia using in-person interviews and, for a subsample, medical records (Popkin, Callies, and others, 1997). We also interviewed front-line providers—doctors, nurses, case managers—at two CMHCs, one in the UPMHP and one outside it, to learn how they perceived issues relating to the delivery of care.

Service Use. At baseline, survey Medicaid beneficiaries with schizophrenia were in frequent contact with the mental health system. Beneficiaries at the UPMHP sites were in poorer health, had more arrests and episodes of victimization, and more inpatient and less outpatient care at the time the program began (Manning and others, 1997). Comparing changes in the services received by beneficiaries with schizophrenia at the UPMHP and non-UPMHP sites, and adjusting for baseline differences, we found no effect on psychiatric hospitalization. There was an early significant difference in change in number of outpatient visits from baseline, but this difference diminished over time and was not statistically significant by the last interview. There was a significant reduction in the percentage of outpatient visits that were for day treatment in the UPMHP group, while the percentages of other types of services, including medication visits, group therapy, and individual therapy, increased over the study period for this group.

Treatment Process. The number of visits for "psychotherapy" fell from baseline to follow-up in both groups, although the decrease was far greater in UPMHP sites. UPMHP beneficiaries were significantly less likely to have a case manager at baseline, but caught up with the non-UPMHP group by the end of the evaluation. In the UPMHP group, the probability of a change in the patient's primary therapist decreased after three years, while it increased in the non-UPMHP group. In contrast, the probability of a patient terminating or being lost to follow-up doubled in the UPMHP group while decreasing by half in the non-UPMHP sites. With respect to medication management, the probability that a patient would receive a suboptimal dose of an antipsychotic medication for a month or longer increased in the UPMHP group and decreased in the non-UPMHP group. Interviews with front-line providers in the UPMHP suggested they felt frustrated, had increased caseloads, and had less time to be proactive when a client was doing poorly. The UPMHP sites appear to have modified their practice patterns in response to the demonstration; fewer changes were seen in the non-UPMHP sites, suggesting a mixed impact on quality of care in the UPMHP (Popkin, Lurie, and others, 1997).

Measures of Outcome

For outcome measures, we calculated "change scores" for each individual (defined as the value of the measure at the follow-up interview minus the value at the baseline interview). In each case, we compared change scores across the UPMHP and non-UPMHP groups. We also analyzed pooled data across all surveys (Manning and others, 1997).

We assessed outcomes with several measures of mental health status: the Global Assessment Scale (GAS), which reports interviewers' assessments of the respondent's overall functioning; two subscales of the Schedule for Affective Disorders and Schizophrenia (SADS), which assess depression; and the Brief Psychiatric Rating Scale (BPRS) including its schizophrenic subscale, which focuses on psychotic symptomatology. UPMHP and non-UPMHP groups differed at baseline on GAS and BPRS measures, with UPMHP beneficiaries reporting worse mental health status. The difference between the groups increased over time because the UPMHP group, on average, improved less than the non-UPMHP group. This finding was most pronounced for the subset of beneficiaries with the worst mental health status at baseline.

We found no impact of the UPMHP on measures of social functioning, general physical health status, or satisfaction with mental health care.

Conclusions

Our analysis of the UPMHP was unique in the comprehensiveness of the measures used, the number of repeated observations, the length of the follow-up period, the integration of qualitative and quantitative research approaches, and the application of a well-known conceptual framework to the evaluation of a managed mental health initiative for Medicaid beneficiaries. Our experience highlights several lessons.

• *Outcomes of clinically relevant subgroups may be as important as the population outcomes overall.* In this demonstration, beneficiaries at UPMHP sites who began the demonstration in the poorest mental health had improved less at the end, compared to those in non-UPMHP sites, but the differences in the population overall were not as pronounced. This finding highlights the importance of focusing on subgroups of interest as well as on the population overall. However, subgroups can be difficult to identify a priori, and their sample sizes can be small, precluding other meaningful analyses.

• *Inherent limitations in real-world evaluation research can make it difficult to interpret specific findings.* Our approach, which used a contemporaneous control group and data collected at multiple points in time, is the strongest design likely to be available for most evaluations of Medicaid managed mental health care initiatives. However, because there was only one pre-UPMHP observation for survey respondents, the possibility exists that significant differences in mental health status may reflect pre-UPMHP trends rather than the impact of the UPMHP. Due to differing health status and utilization patterns between the two groups at baseline, a sophisticated statistical analysis was required to appropriately adjust for baseline differences. Findings from such analyses are often difficult for policymakers and other stakeholders to understand. Finally, medical records data for our entire sample could not be collected because of budget limitations, restricting the subgroup analyses that could be done with these data.

• *The subgroup of beneficiaries that is the focus of the evaluation must be chosen prior to implementation of the initiative, so as to capture baseline data.* Two issues arise with this approach. First, the groups that are the focus of the management efforts of capitated providers may differ. For example, in the UPMHP, managing the use of inpatient care by children and adolescents received considerable attention from CMHCs. Second, the focus of program development on one population may have unintended effects on other subgroups of beneficiaries. It is not feasible to shift the focus to a different subgroup midway through the evaluation, even if the qualitative information collected by researchers suggests that this group is more likely to be affected by the initiative.

We believe it is appropriate to continue to evaluate managed mental health care despite the difficulties. Methodologies for assessing the impact of these initiatives on costs and utilization are relatively well developed, and such analyses can provide useful information for policymakers. While there are inherent limitations in applying standard structure-process-outcome approaches to assessing the impact of managed mental health initiatives on care delivery and patient outcomes in a Medicaid environment, continued work in this area should increase the contribution of evaluation results in shaping future Medicaid reforms.

References

Babigian, A., Mitchell, O., Marshall, P., and Reed, S. "A Mental Health Capitation Experiment: Evaluating the Monroe Livingston Experience." In R. G. Frank and W. G. Manning (eds.), *Economics and Mental Health.* Baltimore: Johns Hopkins University Press, 1992.

Callahan, J. J., Shepard, D. S., Beinecke, R. H., Larson, M., and Cavanaugh, D. "Mental Health/Substance Abuse Treatment in Managed Care: The Massachusetts Medicaid Experience." *Health Affairs,* 1995, *14,* 173–184.

Christianson, J., Gray, D., Kihlstrom, L., and Speckman, Z. "Development of the Utah Prepaid Mental Health Plan." In R. Scheffler and L. Rossiter (eds.), J. Cantor (guest ed.), *Advances in Health Economics and Health Research,* no. 15, Greenwich, Conn.: JAI Press, 1995.

Christianson, J., Manning, W., Lurie, N., Stoner, T., Gray, D., Popkin, M., and Marriott, S. "Utah's Prepaid Mental Health Plan: The First Year." *Health Affairs,* 1995, *14,* 160–172.

Dangerfield, D., and Betit, R. "Managed Mental Health Care in the Public Sector." In W. Goldman and S. Feldman (eds.), *Managed Mental Health Care.* New Directions for Mental Health Services, no. 59, San Francisco: Jossey-Bass, 1993.

Dwyer, D. S., Mitchell, O. S., Cole, R., and Reed, S. K. *Evaluating Mental Health Capitation Treatment: Lessons from Panel Data.* Working Paper 5297. Cambridge, Mass.: National Bureau of Economic Research, 1995.

Essock, S., and Goldman, H. "States' Embrace of Managed Mental Health Care." *Health Affairs,* 1995, *14,* 34–44.

Koyanagi, C. "Mental Health Managed Care: Survey of the States." Washington, D.C.: Bazelon Center for Mental Health Law, 1996.

Leadholm, B., and Kerzner, J. "Implementing a System of Public Managed Care: The Massachusetts Experience." *Behavioral Health Care Tomorrow,* Jul.–Aug. 1993, pp. 36–38.

Lurie, N., Moscovice, I., Popkin, M., and Dysken, M. "Accuracy of Medicaid Claims for Psychiatric Diagnosis: Experience with the Diagnosis of Schizophrenia." *Hospital and Community Psychiatry,* 1992, *43,* 69–71.

Manning, W., Liu, C.-F., Stoner, T., Gray, D., Lurie, N., Popkin, M., and Christianson, J. "Outcomes for Medicaid Beneficiaries with Schizophrenia Under a Prepaid Mental Health Carve-Out." Division of Health Services Research and Policy, School of Public Health, University of Minnesota, 1997.

McGlynn, E. A., Norquist, G. S., Wells, K. B., Sullivan, G., and Liberman, R. P. "Quality-of-Care Research in Mental Health: Responding to the Challenge." *Inquiry,* 1988, *25,* 157–170.

Micali, P., and Nardini, C. "Merit Behavioral Care in Iowa: A Case Study." *Behavioral Health Management,* 1996, *16,* 5–7.

Popkin, M., Callies, A., Lurie, N., Harman, J., Stoner, T., and Manning, W. "An Instrument to Evaluate the Process of Psychiatric Care in Ambulatory Settings." *Psychiatric Services,* 1997, *48,* 524–527.

Popkin, M., Lurie, N., Manning, W., Harman, J., Callies, A., Gray, D., and Christianson, J. "Utah Prepaid Mental Health Plan: Changes in the Process of Care for Medicaid Beneficiaries with Schizophrenia." Minneapolis: Division of Health Services Research and Policy, School of Public Health, University of Minnesota, 1997.

Reed, S., Hennessy, K., Mitchell, O., and Babigian, H. "A Mental Health Capitation Program: II. Cost-Benefit Analysis." *Hospital and Community Psychiatry,* 1994, *45,* 1097–1103.

Schlesinger, M. "On the Limits of Expanding Health Care Reform: Chronic Care in Prepaid Settings." *Milbank Quarterly,* 1986, *64,* 189–215.

Schlesinger, M., and Mechanic, D. "Challenges for Managed Competition from Chronic Illness." *Health Affairs,* 1993, *12* (Suppl.), 123–137.

Stoner, T., Manning, W., Christianson, J., Gray, D., and Marriott, S. "Expenditures for Mental health Services in the Utah Prepaid Mental Health Care Plan." *Health Care Financing Review,* 1997, *18,* 73–93.

"Utah Prepaid Mental Health Plan: 1915(b) Waiver Renewal Request." Division of Health Care Financing, Utah State Department of Health, Salt Lake City, Mar. 15, 1996.

Wright, G. E., and Buck, J. A. "Medicaid Support of Alcohol, Drug Abuse, and Mental Health Services." *Health Care Financing Review,* 1991, *13,* 117–128.

Wyant, D., Christianson, J., and Coleman, B. "The Financial Impact on Community Mental Health Centers of Capitated Contracts with Medicaid: The Utah Prepaid Mental Health Plan." Minneapolis: Division of Health Services Research and Policy, School of Public Health, University of Minnesota, 1997.

NICOLE LURIE *is a professor with the Division of Health Services Research and Policy, School of Public Health, and with the Department of Medicine, School of Medicine, University of Minnesota, Minneapolis.*

JON B. CHRISTIANSON *is a professor with the Division of Health Services Research and Policy, School of Public Health, University of Minnesota, Minneapolis.*

DONALD Z. GRAY *is director of the Research and Evaluation Program, Health Sciences Center, University of Utah, Salt Lake City.*

WILLARD G. MANNING JR. *is a professor with the Department of Health Studies, University of Chicago.*

MICHAEL K. POPKIN *is chief of psychiatry with the Hennepin County Medical Center, Minneapolis, Minnesota.*

Early experience with managed mental health among Colorado Medicaid enrollees who have severe and persistent mental illness indicates that costs can be reduced without negative short-term outcomes.

Managed Mental Health Experience in Colorado

Jaclyn W. Hausman, Neal Wallace, Joan R. Bloom

Is capitation a policy that can result in savings for funders of public mental health services without harming a group of very vulnerable consumers? The State of Colorado implemented a pilot capitation program for Medicaid mental health services in 1995 that begins to address this question. Our research focuses on adults with severe and persistent mental illness because this group may be particularly vulnerable to changes in the financing and delivery of mental health services. Specifically, the evaluation addresses the impact of capitation on a variety of outcomes such as quality of life, physical and mental health status, overall functioning, consumer satisfaction, access to services, and utilization and cost of services. In addition, we examine the impact of capitation on the organizations that provide mental health care to Medicaid recipients, including their structure and culture, service provision, staffing, management information systems (MIS), utilization management (UM) strategies, and coordination of services with other providers (Bloom, 1994). Colorado's pilot program is a particularly interesting example of capitation because it provides two different models of care for comparison with the fee-for-service (FFS) model.

This chapter presents preliminary findings on consumer outcomes and on how services are provided, with a specific focus on how provider organizations and contractors are trying to manage care more efficiently under capitation (Bloom and others, forthcoming).

Background

The public mental health system in Colorado is divided into seventeen service regions. Previously, providers were reimbursed by Medicaid through a fee-for-service payment system. In May 1992, the Colorado State Legislature passed legislation allowing the state to design, implement, and evaluate a pilot program using a prepaid capitated payment system for Medicaid mental health services. This was an attempt both to reduce the escalating cost of services and to improve the delivery and outcomes of mental health services.

Fourteen service regions are included in the capitation pilot program, which began in August and September 1995. The remaining three regions continue to function under the fee-for-service method. Providers in the capitated regions are paid in advance a fixed per-person monthly Medicaid rate. There are two models operating in the regions covered by the capitation pilot program. In Model I, the state has contracts with nonprofit Community Mental Health Centers (CMHCs) who both manage the care and deliver mental health services. There are four capitation contracts that fall within Model I. In Model II, the state has contracts with a joint venture between a single for-profit managed care firm that manages the care and either a single CMHC or an alliance of CMHCs who deliver most of the mental health services in those regions. There are three capitation contracts that fall within this model. All the agencies with contracts are called Mental Health Assessment and Service Agencies (MHASA).

Colorado's program is one of the most inclusive models of capitation that has been evaluated, and thus can serve as a model for other states considering implementing a capitated program. First, the capitation program covers all age groups and includes all inpatient and outpatient mental health services except prescription drugs. Inpatient services include services provided at the state hospitals, except for adults between twenty-two and sixty-four years old. Second, the state does not offer reinsurance or any other measures to protect MHASAs from high-risk clients; the MHASAs bear full financial risk.

Capitation rates paid to MHASAs vary considerably because historical usage was taken into account in the calculation of rates. For example, for fiscal year 1995–96, the range across MHASAs for Old Age Pension (OAP-A) is $1.31 to $27.04 per member per month, and for Aid to the Needy Disabled, Old Age Pension (OAP-B), and Aid to the Blind, the range is $23.84 to $156.54 per member per month. The total amounts paid to each MHASA must meet federal and state regulations. Federal regulations require that total expenditures under capitation cannot exceed the amount that would have been paid for the same group of Medicaid recipients under a fee-for-service model, while state regulations require that total expenditures cannot exceed 95 percent of what would have been paid under fee-for-service.

Impact on Individual Consumers

In this evaluation, a sample of consumers receiving services under the two models of capitation are compared with each other and with a sample of consumers receiving services under the FFS model. Study subjects were restricted to adults over the age of eighteen with a diagnosis of either schizophrenia or bipolar affective disorder, or at least one twenty-four-hour inpatient stay in the year prior to the beginning of the study. Seventy-five percent of the sample had contact with the mental health system in the year prior to the implementation of capitation, while the remaining 25 percent were new enrollees after the implementation of capitation. The total number of subjects in this study is 683. The sample currently available for analysis is 511: 188 subjects from Model I, 179 from Model II, and 148 subjects from the FFS area.

Each subject is being interviewed in person every six months during the course of the study (for a total of five interviews anticipated by the end of the evaluation). The subjects are asked questions about their physical and mental health status, their quality of life including housing, finances, social and family relationships, and satisfaction with and access to mental health services. Individual-level data on Medicaid and state hospital utilization and cost of services come from three data sources. Medicaid claims tapes provided Medicaid service data for all service regions prior to capitation, and continue to provide data for the noncapitated service regions after capitation. Comparable data on Medicaid services in the capitated regions after capitation was implemented come from a "shadow billing" system developed by the state. State hospital service data are provided directly by the state hospitals.

In this preliminary analysis, Medicaid service costs and utilization are reported in three aggregate categories: total, inpatient, and outpatient. Inpatient cost and utilization include both community and state hospital services. Cost and outcomes were analyzed using multiple regression techniques. The purpose of these analyses was to identify changes in service patterns and patient outcomes in the two capitated service areas just prior to and after implementation of the capitation program, relative to the FFS area. This process assures that any changes found can be attributed to the implementation of capitation alone and not to general trends in the provision or performance of public mental health services in Colorado. Additionally, the analyses controlled for differences in the sociodemographic characteristics of the sample clients, including age, sex, ethnicity, and prior service use, to assure that the identified effects are not due to variation in the backgrounds of severely mentally ill individuals sampled within each service area. The specific periods of analysis were October 1994 through June 1995 and October 1995 through June 1996. The three-month period July–September 1995 was excluded because phased implementation of capitation was occurring then.

The best overall measure of cost performance is the average cost per person, including persons who receive no services in a period. To accurately estimate the cost per person from the sample data, a two-step procedure was used. Separate regression analyses were employed to estimate the probability that a person received services and the average cost of services provided to each user of services. Estimates of the probability of use and the cost per user were computed for each of the three service areas in each of the two (pre-and postcapitation) time periods. The product of the estimated probability of use and cost per user provides an appropriate estimate of the cost per person. This analytic process was completed for each of the three aggregate service categories: total, inpatient, and outpatient.

Initially both Model I and Model II areas had higher total service costs per person than the FFS area. After capitation, FFS increased, Model I stayed level, and Model II declined significantly. If we assume that FFS represents the secular or general trend in mental health provision without capitation, then both Model I and Model II can be said to decline relative to FFS (Model I stays flat while FFS is rising).

Model I initially had higher outpatient cost per person and lower inpatient cost per person than FFS. After capitation, the Model I area had reduced both outpatient and inpatient cost per person relative to FFS, but maintained the initial investment pattern in inpatient and outpatient services. The Model II area began with higher outpatient and inpatient cost per person relative to FFS and had reductions in both service categories after capitation, yielding both outpatient and inpatient costs per person at or below the FFS area. Thus, while both capitated areas reduced inpatient and outpatient cost per person relative to FFS, the extent of the change was much greater in the Model II area.

There are similarities in the types of changes that occurred for the cost per user and probability of use in the two capitated areas, and the proportional change relative to FFS. They are applied, however, to very different initial conditions, yielding different net results. Specifically, both areas had similar proportional reductions in inpatient cost per user and the probability of outpatient use compared to the FFS area. However, since Model I had higher outpatient and lower inpatient cost and use than Model II initially, the similar proportional reductions have a much greater net effect in the Model II area.

The analysis of outcome data controls for variation in client characteristics across service areas. For the vast majority of the seventeen outcome measures that we selected in both Model I and II, there are very few statistically significant changes. Considering the short time frame of this preliminary analysis, we believe that a conclusion of "no change" in short-term clinical outcomes is the best statement regarding overall results.

Management of Utilization Within Provider Organizations

Capitation introduces incentives to manage care more efficiently, as providers are given a specified monthly payment in advance for each Medicaid enrollee rather than being reimbursed retroactively for each service provided. Consequently, providers may change the way they manage the care of consumers. For example, without capitation, there may not be any limits on the amount of services that a consumer may receive. In addition, under FFS, outpatient providers (such as CMHCs) have no financial incentives to try to reduce or minimize use of inpatient services. With capitation, providers and payers may try to restrict admissions both for inpatient and outpatient services, introduce strategies to reduce lengths of stay and intensity of services provided, introduce benefit limits, and change staffing patterns to reduce costs.

Prior to the implementation of capitation, CMHCs employed very limited utilization management strategies. No CMHC required preauthorization for outpatient services, although several required preauthorization for inpatient services. Very few had an initial assessment of length of service, and only one or two claimed that they initiated utilization management strategies at intake. Most CMHCs did conduct some level of preadmission screening and used the state definitions of target populations to develop admissions criteria. Only a few stated that these criteria were written and that they had established training and education mechanisms to ensure that staff were aware of these criteria. In addition, there were no benefit limits for Medicaid consumers at any CMHC. During the first set of interviews, staff at several of the CMHCs did state they were developing strategies for utilization management, such as preauthorization, in anticipation of capitation.

After the implementation of capitation, MHASAs began to develop and implement utilization management strategies in the effort to reduce the cost of providing services to Medicaid recipients. The three joint ventures in Model II have similar policies and procedures with regard to managing the care of consumers. Consumers may enter the system either from a central service center operated by the managed care company or through the CMHCs. The service center is financially responsible for all inpatient services, and must be contacted by any other provider (that is, contractors such as CMHCs and other network providers) for preauthorization of any inpatient services. The CMHCs bear the financial risk for outpatient services (excluding services provided by network providers).

There is little variation within Model II on how inpatient services are managed. Providers have adopted strategies to reduce both hospital admissions and lengths of stay. Within CMHCs, utilization management teams identify high-risk consumers and maintain close contact with them to be aware of signs of psychiatric decompensation. One CMHC referred to its program as a "hospital without walls." At that particular CMHC a consumer may have up to twelve home visits per week to prevent hospitalization. Intensive case management, medication monitoring, and acute treatment units (ATUs) that provide twenty-four-hour care are some of the other strategies being used to reduce hospital admissions.

Efforts are also made to reduce the lengths of stay. Discharge planning is begun upon admission, and there are service center staff within the state hospital. There is some concern that efforts to reduce lengths of stay will result in higher rates of recidivism.

There are no benefit limits established for outpatient services in Model II. Initially, consumers were granted ten outpatient visits without preauthorization; after these visits reauthorization could be requested from the service center. Our data suggest that reauthorization is generally granted, and that conflicts between the clinician and the Service Center are rare and easily resolved. At the time of our last interviews (Fall 1996), interviewees indicated that the ten-visit initial limit was being eliminated because reauthorization was always granted.

Interviewees from Model II suggest that outpatient utilization is not being tracked as closely as inpatient utilization, and that utilization management strategies to provide outpatient services more efficiently are insufficient. In addition, there is greater variation within Model II in the extent to which utilization management policies are in place because they are developed within CMHCs or the MHASA. Some provider organizations appear to have internal utilization teams that review cases, conduct concurrent reviews, and work with clinicians to develop more effective treatment plans and strategies, whereas others seem to be operating in a less structured fashion. There was general agreement across CMHCs within Model II that management of outpatient services needed improvement.

There is potential for greater variation within Model I because there are four MHASAs operating independently, with no common management or organizational structure. Data from two of the MHASAs have been examined in order to compare and contrast different ways of managing care under capitation. Both are freestanding CMHCs with capitation contracts with the state. Both MHASAs appear to be using similar strategies to reduce outpatient utilization, such as preadmission screening and concurrent review. Both also require preauthorization for inpatient referrals and admissions. Early intervention and increased contact with consumers through intensive case management and ATUs are strategies that both employ to reduce use of inpatient services. One MHASA also tries to use financial leverage with contract hospitals to reduce lengths of stay.

Neither MHASA has instituted strict benefit limits, although one MHASA allows ten visits initially and requires reauthorization within six months. While reauthorization is typically granted, less intensive, and therefore less costly, treatment strategies may be suggested. There was some concern that while the reauthorization process appeared to be working well, quiet consumers may not be getting what they need due to the squeaky wheel syndrome. Thus, while both Models I and II have adopted strategies to reduce inpatient utilization, according to interview data, Model I appears to be doing more to manage outpatient utilization than Model II (this finding applies only to CMHC providers in Model II; network providers are not included).

Discussion

The purpose of this study is to identify any short-term changes in the process or outcome of the provision of public mental health services to severely mentally ill individuals in Colorado following the implementation of a capitated payment system. Interviews with key informants suggest that while both Models I and II have adopted similar strategies to reduce inpatient admissions and decrease lengths of stay, Model I has adopted more strategies to manage outpatient care than Model II. Despite the differences in their management strategies, it is interesting to note that the proportional effect of capitation on service provision in the two service areas is very similar.

After capitation was implemented, both capitated areas had similar proportional reductions in the probability of service use relative to the FFS area, with the strongest change in outpatient service use. Additionally, both capitated areas had similar proportional reductions in inpatient cost per user compared to FFS. Prior to capitation, however, the Model I area had lower inpatient and higher outpatient cost and use than either Model II or the FFS areas. Thus the differences in outpatient service management appear to reflect alignment with the initial conditions of service provision rather than differences in organizational form.

Despite the similar proportional changes in service provision, the combination of these changes with the different initial conditions yielded a much larger net change in the total service cost per person for Model II. Since Model II had higher initial levels of inpatient use, the proportional reduction in the average inpatient cost per user resulted in much greater total savings.

Two potential policy conclusions can be drawn. First, there are no apparent differences in the short-term responses to capitation by the two different organizational forms represented by Models I and II, if we control for initial conditions. Second, uniform implementation of capitation does not imply uniform local effects. Initial differences in local conditions of service provision may largely determine the choice of management response and the total amount (as opposed to the proportional amount) of changes in utilization and cost.

Clinical outcomes and satisfaction had little overall change. For the short term, it can be concluded that capitation can reduce service cost per person without significant change in clinical status. This result is consistent with the view that FFS payment systems may encourage the provision of types and amounts of service that exceed their return in clinical and quality-of-life outcomes. Capitation, on the other hand, provides risks and incentives to encourage a closer match between the marginal costs and the marginal benefits of services provided to each individual. Thus, in a change from FFS to capitation, reductions in service use may occur without commensurate reductions in outcomes. This may include, over short periods, a reduction from some to no services provided. This analysis does include persons who do not receive services in either one or both of the nine-month pre- and postcapitation periods. Our analyses indicate no differences in outcome change for these subgroups compared to those consistently receiving services. Thus the study results suggest that changes under capitation in decisions about whether to provide services and how much services to provide may not be inconsistent with consumers' clinical needs.

Two important considerations follow from the combined cost and outcome results. First, to the extent that these short-term results hold over time, they imply that some excess service quality existed in Colorado prior to capitation. From a policy perspective, the relative success of capitation in Colorado cannot be extrapolated to its application in other service systems without reference to specific local initial conditions. Second, the validity of these results beyond the short term are largely dependent upon the assumption that (measurable) individual outcome changes occur simultaneously with changes in service provision, which may not be the case. Analysis of the complete data from this study spanning a two-year postcapitation period is necessary to validate these short-term results.

References

Bloom, J. R. "Capitating Medicaid Mental Health Services." Health and Human Services, National Institute of Mental Health Grant Number MH54136, 1994.

Bloom, J. R., Hu, T. W., Wallace, N., Cuffel, B., Hausman, J., and Scheffler, R. "Mental Health Costs and Outcomes Under Alternative Capitation Systems in Colorado: Early Results." *Journal of Mental Health Policy and Economics*, forthcoming.

JACLYN W. HAUSMAN *is a doctoral student in health services and policy analysis at the University of California, Berkeley.*

NEAL WALLACE *is a doctoral student in health services and policy analysis at the University of California, Berkeley.*

JOAN R. BLOOM *is a professor of public health at the University of California, Berkeley.*

Medicaid managed care experience in Massachusetts indicates that
costs can be contained without harmful effects, but future
developments will still need careful monitoring.

Managed Mental Health Experience in Massachusetts

Barbara Dickey, Edward C. Norton, Sharon-Lise T. Normand,
Hocine Azeni, William H. Fisher

In 1992, Massachusetts was the first state to receive a 1915b waiver from the Health Care Financing Administration, requiring all Medicaid beneficiaries to enroll in a local HMO or to select a Medicaid-approved primary care clinician (PCC). Virtually all psychiatrically disabled beneficiaries chose the latter arrangement. Under the PCC plan, Medicaid contracted with a single proprietary vendor to manage the delivery of all Medicaid-reimbursed mental health benefits. The managed care vendor pursued four specific cost-containment strategies: negotiation of lower reimbursement rates with a network of providers, implementation of an aggressive utilization management plan, development of community-based alternatives to hospitalization, and development of a statewide network of general and private psychiatric hospitals. These hospitals gained access to the vendor's beneficiary population in return for acceptance of a reduced, all-inclusive daily rate.

Under the terms of its contract, the vendor was required to make available all behavioral health services, including acute inpatient treatment, crisis stabilization, outpatient evaluation and treatment, psychiatric day treatment, residential detoxification, and methadone treatment. The vendor was directed to add diversionary services, including acute residential treatment programs, family stabilization, and partial hospitalization programs. The vendor was also

Note: This research was supported by the National Institute of Mental Health grant RO–1 MH54076. The authors acknowledge editorial support from Lydia Ratcliff.

responsible for utilization review, claims processing, systems support, provider relations, and decentralized regional case management and network oversight. The contract excluded payment for long-term nursing home care, nonreimbursable mental health support services provided by the Massachusetts Department of Mental Health (DMH), treatment for medical disorders, and outpatient pharmacy. In addition, it excluded members of HMOs and those with Medicaid as a second insurer. The vendor was paid a capitation rate for disabled beneficiaries almost four times that for nondisabled. In turn, the vendor paid providers on a fee-for-service basis. The contract with the managed care company specified that its financial risk would be limited to $1 million in profit or loss, which was defined as the *risk corridor*. In subsequent years Medicaid and the vendor agreed to some adjustments in the capitation rate and the risk corridor of the contract. In this chapter we describe three aspects of the Massachusetts initiative: formation of the provider networks, shifts in the patterns of care and their associated costs, and cost shifting to other state agencies.

The Managed Care Provider Network: Selective Contracting

The first task of the vendor was to contract with a group of providers selected competitively. They would be the sole providers of reimbursed treatment. We studied the network selective contracting process, using data from the Massachusetts Health Data Consortium and the 1991 American Hospital Association survey of hospitals, as well as paid claims data from the Department of Medical Assistance (Medicaid) and the managed care vendor. In addition to the quantitative data, we interviewed administrators from both winning and losing hospitals to learn more about the procurement process. Of the 118 eligible Massachusetts hospitals, 57 (48 percent) actually made bids. Of these, 37 (65 percent) were selected by the vendor to be part of the statewide network. Seven of these were freestanding psychiatric hospitals whose exclusion from treating adult (age eighteen to sixty-four) Medicaid patients was waived. Five public hospitals, 7 for-profit and 45 nonprofit hospitals were included in the network.

Hospital Network Selection. Mental health advocates feared that price rather than quality would be the overriding factor in hospital selection. Our analysis suggested, however, that factors related to quality (for example, experience with the psychiatrically disabled and Medicaid populations) were among the most significant predictors of network selection. Cost, as measured by a hospital's pre-network per diem reimbursement rate, was not a significant predictor of network inclusion (Fisher, Lindrooth, Norton, and Dickey, 1997). A second indicator that cost was not the only factor was the selection of eight major teaching hospitals for inclusion in the network.

Competition. The vendor was contractually obligated to develop a network that would ensure convenient access to hospitals throughout the state. The result of this mandate was that psychiatric bed supply in the region in which a hospital was located was a significant inverse predictor of the probability of winning a contract: more beds in the region reduced the likelihood of winning. In the heavily bedded metropolitan Boston area, for example, competition for inclusion was intense; only ten of the seventeen Boston area hospitals entering bids were selected. But in the less densely bedded regions in western Massachusetts, all seven hospitals entering bids gained membership. This pattern, consistent with that found in earlier research on competitive bidding for community-based services (Schlesinger, Dorwart, and Pulice, 1986), calls into question the notion that competition can always be relied upon as a major contributor to cost savings in managed care or as an incentive to improve quality.

Administrator Perceptions. Preliminary findings from interviews with administrators in network hospitals, particularly those having less experience with managed care, suggested problems with the process of creating an internal utilization review mechanism to meet the requirements of the vendor, excessive paperwork, and universal dissatisfaction over slow reimbursement by the vendor. Most of the administrators acknowledged the negotiated per diem as adequate.

Our interviews also suggested that the selective contracting mechanism had implications for nonmember hospitals as well. Administrators saw their failure to become part of the network leading to serious competitive disadvantage. Some experienced the erosion of their business. Others noted that Medicaid beneficiaries continued to come to their emergency rooms, taking up capacity and often receiving treatment while transfer to a network hospital could be arranged. This care was not reimbursed by the vendor, however, which placed an additional financial burden on the non-network hospital.

Patterns of Care and Costs for the Seriously Mentally Ill

Managed care is expected to change how enrollees use services, especially inpatient treatment. We chose to study changes in patterns of care and related expenditures for vulnerable high-risk enrollees because they have been the subject of concern by critics of managed care and are likely to have the highest expenditures. We studied all adult disabled Massachusetts Medicaid beneficiaries, aged eighteen to sixty-four years, for whom a reimbursement claim was submitted for treatment of a major mental illness (ICD-9-CM primary code of 295–299) at least once during 1991 and 1992 (prior to managed care) and 1994 and 1995 (after the introduction of managed care). Because the seriously mentally ill are sometimes treated in state hospitals, we also merged state hospital admissions data from Department of Mental Health inpatient files with the Medicaid claims to provide a complete picture of treatment patterns. Details of the methods used to create the database are reported elsewhere (Dickey and others, 1995; Dickey and others, 1996). Length of stay for hospitalizations and expenditures were calculated as an average of both acute general hospital episode days *and* state hospital episode days (treatment not reimbursed by Medicaid). All expenditure figures are reported in 1995 dollars by adjusting expenditures for inflation using the gross domestic product deflator (U.S. Department of Commerce, 1995).

Access. The largest observed difference between the pre and post managed care cohorts is in the increased number of enrollees treated under managed care (up about 25 percent). This increase suggests that access to care was not curtailed after the introduction of managed care. We should note that over this period the number of enrolled disabled beneficiaries increased in Massachusetts as it did in other states. Overall rates of access thus may have remained essentially constant, but are unlikely to have declined. The sociodemographic and diagnostic characteristics of both cohorts were similar, although nontrivial shifts upward were observed in the proportion with Substance Use Disorder and in treatment for major affective disorders post managed care.

Mental Health Service Utilization Patterns. Inpatient admissions to general hospitals or DMH state hospitals declined substantially, from 26 percent to 20 percent of those treated after managed care was introduced, but the mean length of stay remained unchanged (about thirty-one days per episode). There was a small reduction in the median length of stay (fifteen days before and twelve days after). Both DMH and Medicaid annual bed-days, as a rate for enrollees treated, dropped substantially post managed care, a function of the reduced number of admissions. If the managed care vendor had shifted inpatient treatment to the (non–managed care) DMH state hospitals, overall admission rates might have stayed the same or increased, and length of stay might have increased. Enrollees with schizophrenia, who had the highest rate of admission to general or state hospitals pre managed care, 30 percent annually, dropped to 25 percent annually.

Continuity of Care. We examined treatment post hospital discharge to assess continuity of care by categorizing every discharge into one of four categories: whether or not follow-up care was provided within thirty days and whether or not rehospitalization occurred within thirty days. We found that the overall distribution of follow-up care did not change, but the proportion of admissions followed by a rehospitalization did increase slightly (from 22.1 percent to 23.2 percent) post managed care. Although this suggests a possible reduction in continuity of care, the total number of readmissions post managed care was reduced by one thousand. Thus it is likely that those admitted in 1994 and 1995 were more disturbed than those pre managed care, a condition that probably increased the odds of readmission. That 30 percent of admissions pre managed care and 34 percent post managed care had no claim for professional follow-up treatment is cause for concern, although throughout both study periods, it is possible that some patients seen in day programs and residential settings had professional evaluations not reimbursed by Medicaid and did not appear in the claims database.

We also summarized continuity of care data by sociodemographic and clinical characteristics, which reveal good news about two racial groups with significant language barriers to care. Asian Americans and Latinos in Massachusetts had the highest aftercare follow-up and the lowest readmission rates of any racial groups. These data must be cautiously interpreted, however, because it is also true that the rates of treatment for these two groups were significantly lower than one would expect, in view of their representation in the general population. Both before and after managed care, younger enrollees (eighteen to forty-four) accounted for 75 percent of the discharges; females had the larger number of admissions, the higher proportion of follow-up care, *and* the higher proportion of readmissions within thirty days of discharge.

Assessment of Expenditures. Average annual mental health expenditures per treated Medicaid enrollee fell by about 25 percent following introduction of managed care, from about $11,000 to just over $8,200. These costs are the sum of both Medicaid and DMH expenditures. For those with at least one inpatient admission, costs fell by only about 10 percent, but the fraction receiving such care fell by more than 20 percent. Combined reductions in the price and utilization of inpatient care were the chief factors responsible for limiting total expenditures.

Cost Shifting

The political impetus to implement Medicaid managed care programs comes largely from the desire to control expenditures. Therefore, an important criterion for evaluating Medicaid managed care is the extent to which savings were in fact realized. This is a difficult research question, in part because funding for behavioral health care comes from several sources. There would be no savings if costs were simply shifted to other state programs. Most states operate hospitals serving the mentally ill exclusively but fund these facilities separately from their Medicaid programs. DMH hospitals treat Medicaid beneficiaries with severe behavior management problems, but cannot bill Medicaid for these services. Therefore, managed care may induce cost shifting across public funding sources from Medicaid to DMH, which may distort simple calculations of cost savings. We also examined cost shifting to non–mental health Medicaid reimbursed services (such as treatment for medical disorders) and to DMH state hospitals (Norton, Lindroth, and Dickey, 1997a, 1997b) using paid claims from the Department of Medical Assistance (Medicaid) and the Department of Mental Health. These data included expenditures not covered by the vendor (state hospital treatment, treatment of medical disorders, and pharmaceuticals) as well as reimbursed treatment costs for psychiatric and substance use disorders managed by the vendor. We tested whether expenditures for the services covered by the vendor would decrease and the other services not covered by the vendor would increase after the introduction of managed care.

Cost Shifting and Savings. DMH expenditures for hospitalization of the seriously mentally ill declined, suggesting that costs were not shifted to DMH. The data suggest that they might have been shifted to the medical and pharmacy benefits, which had per-person increases after the implementation of managed care. However, examination of the pharmacy data reveal that increased per-person costs were a function of higher pharmacy prices rather than increases in the number of pharmacy claims. It is possible that the increases in medical expenditures were the result of cost shifting. Nevertheless, the per-person total expenditures, including medical and pharmacy costs, were down about 5 percent after managed care, suggesting that if cost shifting was in fact occurring, overall expenditures were still lower than before. Savings appeared greatest for beneficiaries in the highest quartile of expenditures.

Discussion

Massachusetts is an important case study because it was the first state to implement a statewide managed behavioral care program for all Medicaid beneficiaries. Evaluations of managed behavioral health care plans are in an early stage of development, however, and little descriptive information is available to provide benchmarks against which to compare different approaches to cost containment (Schlesinger, 1986, 1989; Callahan and others, 1994; Wells, Astrakhan, Tischler, and Unutzer, 1995). The Massachusetts experience is an indicator of what may be happening in other states that have followed Massachusetts down this particular managed care path (single proprietary vendor, a network of providers competitively bid, and utilization review for network providers paid on a fee-for-service basis). Data are needed from other states before coming to firm conclusions.

Positive findings in our study outweighed negative ones. The approach to cost-containment was effective in reducing expenditures for disabled beneficiaries' mental health care, primarily by limiting the price and utilization of inpatient hospital treatment. It also appears that savings derived from managed care were not achieved by shifting costs to the state mental health agency, as some had feared. Moreover, the prediction by some observers that quality of care would be compromised in favor of cost savings might be countered, to at least some extent, by our finding that hospitals' experience with the beneficiary population was a more important factor than price in predicting a hospital's inclusion in the vendor network. Historically many providers have been reluctant to treat the seriously mentally ill, but in our study roughly half of the hospitals eligible to bid did so. This level of interest was sufficient to develop a managed care network that served both AFDC and disabled (SSI) aid categories. But competition existed only in densely populated urban areas. Furthermore, to the extent that administrative data measure access to treatment and continuity of care post discharge, we found no evidence that access to treatment had been limited and observed only very small shifts in the patterns of post-discharge follow-up care.

Our study of cost shifting highlights the potential problem of containing costs in one state agency when they might be shifted to other agencies. Viewed from a global perspective, managed care in the public sector may have trouble achieving the goal of overall cost reduction if there are multiple sources of public funding inviting cost shifting. Our data also suggest that policies will be more effective in reducing or shifting expenditures when the targeted population has above-average pre–managed care expenditures.

In addition to studies of the intended effects of managed care, such as the reduction of inappropriate use of services and the reduction in expenditures, it is widely believed that a number of secondary effects may also occur, such as a shift in enrollee case-mix consistent with financial incentives. If capitation is the mode of paying for mental health services, it would benefit managed care companies financially if they were able to enroll beneficiaries who were older and were less seriously ill (both groups are at lower risk for hospitalization). An increase in beneficiaries with such characteristics would likely result in a financial windfall for the managed care company. This can only be avoided by minimizing categorical exceptions to managed care enrollment and by having enrollment eligibility standards determined and monitored by Medicaid, not by the managed care company.

Although this study has provided much useful information on shifts in patterns of care and expenditures in Massachusetts, much remains to be investigated. To cite just two key areas for research: we must gather clinical information on enrollees that will permit us to speak more confidently about quality of care as measured by enrollee outcomes. We also need to disentangle the multiple factors associated with change by using longitudinal analyses that take account of changing case-mix as well as the managed care intervention to distinguish between course of illness, the introduction of new medications, and the effects of managed care.

References

Callahan, J. J., Shepard, D. S., Beinecke, R. H., Larson, M. J., and Cavanaugh, D. "Evaluation of the Massachusetts Medicaid Mental Health/Substance Abuse Program." Report submitted to *Massachusetts Division of Medical Assistance,* Jan. 1994.

Dickey, B., Norton, E. C., Normand, S. L., Azeni, H., Fisher, W., and Altaffer, F. "Massachusetts Medicaid Managed Health Care Reform: Treatment for the Psychiatrically Disabled." *Advances in Health Economics,* 1995, *15,* 99–116.

Dickey, B., Normand, S. L., Azeni, H., Fisher, W., and Altaffer, F. "Managing the Care of Schizophrenia: Lessons from a 4–year Massachusetts Medicaid Study." *Archives of General Psychiatry,* 1996, *53,* 945–952.

Fisher, W. H., Lindrooth, R. C., Norton, E. C., and Dickey, B. "How Managed Care Organizations Develop Selective Contracting Networks for Psychiatric Inpatient Care: A Case Study." Unpublished manuscript, under review, 1997.

Norton, E. C., Lindrooth, R. C., and Dickey, B. "Cost-Shifting in Managed Care." Unpublished manuscript, 1997a.

Norton, E. C., Lindrooth, R. C., and Dickey, B. "Cost-Shifting in a Mental Health Carve-Out for the AFDC Population." *Health Care Financing Review,* 1997b, *18,* 95–108.

Schlesinger, M. "On the Limits of Expanding Health Care Reform: Chronic Care in Prepaid Settings." *Milbank Quarterly,* 1986, *64,* 189–215.

Schlesinger, M. "Striking a Balance: Capitation, the Mentally Ill, and Public Policy." In D. Mechanic and L. H. Aiken (eds.), *Paying for Services: Promises and Pitfalls of Capitation.* New Directions for Mental Health Services, no. 43. San Francisco: Jossey-Bass, 1989.

Schlesinger, M., Dorwart, R. A., and Pulice, R. "Competitive Bidding and States' Purchase of Services: The Case of Mental Health in Massachusetts." *Journal of Policy Analysis and Management,* 1986, *5,* 245–263.

U.S. Department of Commerce. *Survey of Current Business.* Washington D.C.: Government Printing Office, 1995.

Wells, K. B., Astrakhan, B. M., Tischler, G. L., and Unutzer, J. "Issues and Approaches in Evaluating Managed Mental Health Care." *Milbank Quarterly,* 1995, *73,* 57–75.

BARBARA DICKEY is associate professor, Department of Psychiatry, Harvard Medical School, and director, Department of Mental Health Services Research at McLean Hospital in Belmont, Massachusetts.

EDWARD C. NORTON is assistant professor, Department of Health Policy and Administration, School of Public Health, University of North Carolina, Chapel Hill.

SHARON-LISE T. NORMAND is assistant professor, Department of Health Care Policy, Harvard Medical School, and Department of Biostatistics, Harvard School of Public Health.

HOCINE AZENI is senior analyst, Department of Mental Health Services Research, McLean Hospital, Belmont, Massachusetts.

WILLIAM H. FISHER is associate professor, Department of Psychiatry, and director, Center for Psychosocial and Forensic Services Research, University of Massachusetts Medical School, Worcester.

PART FOUR

The Future of Behavioral Health

A thoughtful regulatory framework is needed to guide the evolution of the behavioral health care industry and to encourage high performance standards.

The Future of Behavioral Health

David Mechanic

In September 1997, the National Alliance for the Mentally Ill (NAMI) issued its first report card on managed care, rating the industry on nine major measures and providing more detailed profiles of performance on the largest behavioral health care companies (Hall, Edgar, and Flynn, 1997). In NAMI's view, while there was variability among companies on some of the criteria, the industry failed on all of them.

NAMI set a high standard for mental health services systems. Its criteria asked whether behavioral health care companies had up-to-date treatment guidelines, whether they provided adequate inpatient care, whether they made available assertive case management teams, and whether patients had ready access to the most effective new, but expensive, medications. The criteria also examined how the companies handle suicide attempts, whether they involve consumers and family members in care, the use of outcome measures to make policy, accessibility to rehabilitation services, and the assurance of stable housing.

In fairness to behavioral health care companies, however, very few mental health systems prior to behavioral health care could meet these standards—as some of NAMI's earlier report cards on the state systems readily illustrate. NAMI defines reasonable goals and standards, but achieving these goals is not solely under the control of managed care. Unless purchasers are prepared to pay for assertive community treatment, rehabilitation, family psychoeducation, appropriate housing, job training, or whatever, it is unrealistic to expect that these services will be easily accessible. If patients are to routinely receive new drugs that are of increased effectiveness or have less disturbing side-effects despite cost differences that are ten or twentyfold, then purchasers must be willing to provide capitated payments that reflect these costs. If business goes simply to the lowest bidder, purchasers would be foolish to expect the level of care that NAMI demands.

When the purchaser is a public agency representing the most vulnerable clients, those who negotiate contracts have a special responsibility to set standards for service explicitly and precisely. But it is naive to believe that the issue is simply one of writing careful contracts or even monitoring performance to ensure appropriate access and quality. State mental health officials also operate under executive and legislative budgetary constraints and cannot simply demand all valuable services whatever the cost. What such officials can demand in a contract depends on what the program is prepared to pay, and this in turn depends on broader mental health politics and the competition between mental health and other areas for public financial support. As managed behavioral health becomes a dominant force in the marketplace it becomes an easy target to blame for failures, some justifiably and others not.

The behavioral health care industry developed because purchasers found its claims that it could eliminate waste and provide care more effectively credible. While it has substantially demonstrated the former, the cost-effectiveness of managed behavioral health care remains an open question. Most of the cost reductions come from shortening inpatient length of stay—but unless such reductions are accompanied by strong systems of community care we have little reason to feel optimistic. As the chapters in this volume indicate, mental health outcomes are more difficult to measure than general health care outcomes, and costs can easily and often invisibly be shifted to other sectors including family life, the workplace, social services, and the criminal justice system.

The public outcry about behavioral health care, and managed care more generally, is already eliciting a strong regulatory response. Managed care offers a field day to politicians who want to please concerned constituents with little political risk. The practices of some managed care companies, more interested in the quick dollar than in building a foundation of public trust and confidence, provide the media with horror stories that stimulate and support regulatory efforts of varying merit. Legislation is repeatedly introduced that seeks to specify the formation of practice networks, access to specialists, the qualifications of utilization reviewers, the requirements before denying care, and the minimum number of visits and inpatient days for varying mental health conditions. Some of these regulatory initiatives are seat-of-the-pants efforts, untested, and of dubious value. Some will simply increase cost without adding greater value or subject plans and providers to increased bureaucratic burdens. Having legislators micromanaging mental health care is even more frightening than having MBAs doing so.

We will no doubt develop a more meaningful regulatory framework with time and experience and not simply react to the latest anecdote publicized by the media. The industry is already substantially consolidating, with companies concerned not only with present profits but also long-term industry standing. It is alleged that the fly-by-night companies are disappearing, though that proposition is not easily tested. In any case, some mental health advocates worry that as the remaining companies get larger and dominate the market, state-level administrators will be no match for them in sophistication and expertise and will have difficulty in successfully bargaining with them. Similarly, as these companies grow and gain increased influence they can develop considerable capacity to affect mental health politics. NAMI and other consumer and professional organizations are thus an important countervailing influence in keeping client needs in the forefront of public discussion and negotiation.

There are many who would hope that the behavioral health care industry would just go away. But the influences that led to its emergence will increase and accelerate in the coming years. There are those who strongly believe that it is inappropriate for investors to make profits on behavioral health care and that if care must be managed, it should be managed within a nonprofit, community-oriented ethic. Others simply worry that with the need to please investors, companies and their activities must grow even when this is not in the interests of their clients or effective performance. Still others wonder whether the mental health dollar is sufficiently large to pay management costs and dividends and also provide high-quality service. These questions are all ideological and almost impossible to resolve.

The NAMI standards are helpful in beginning to define those areas that need careful attention, contractual negotiation, and continuing monitoring. They also help make explicit value choices and economic considerations in contracting processes. If capitation rates are too low to guarantee ready availability to the new, expensive medications, as some managed care executives argue, then perhaps this has to be examined in relation to the range of profits within the existing capitation rates. If we expect behavioral health care to make arrangements for housing, family psychosocial education, and vocational rehabilitation, do contracts clearly define these expectations and do capitation rates realistically reflect such coverage? Accurately predicting resource use among persons with serious mental illness remains a significant problem and until we have improved measures to adjust capitation rates much uncertainty and gaming behavior will continue.

We can predict that behavioral health care as we know it will be very different five or ten years from now. Consolidation will continue, and fewer companies will operate in a more highly regulated environment. Standards of care and performance measures will be much better developed and the quality of care will be monitored more carefully and intensively. In all likelihood, most mental health professionals will accommodate to managed care practices and more routinely use disease management approaches and practice guidelines. The evidence is overwhelming that the mental health professions are still far from meeting even minimal standards for treating major mental illnesses such as schizophrenia or major depression. Conventional practice has been extraordinarily difficult to change. The promise of managed care is that behavioral health managers and mental health professionals will cooperate together, in a constructive regulatory environment, to bring mental health practice closer to a high standard and in accord with developing scientific evidence.

Reference

Hall, L. L., Edgar, E. R., and Flynn, L. M. *Stand and Deliver: Action Call to a Failing Industry. The NAMI Managed Care Report Card.* Arlington, Va.: National Alliance for the Mentally Ill, 1997.

DAVID MECHANIC *is director of the Institute for Health, Health Care Policy, and Aging Research and René Dubos University Professor of Behavioral Science, Rutgers University.*

INDEX

ORDERING INFORMATION

NEW DIRECTIONS FOR MENTAL HEALTH SERVICES is a series of paperback books that presents timely and readable volumes on subjects of concern to clinicians, administrators, and others involved in the care of the mentally disabled. Each volume is devoted to one topic and includes a broad range of authoritative articles written by noted specialists in the field. Books in the series are published quarterly in Fall, Winter, Spring, and Summer and are available for purchase by subscription and individually.

SUBSCRIPTIONS cost $63.00 for individuals (a savings of 27 percent over single-copy prices) and $105.00 for institutions, agencies, and libraries. Standing orders are accepted. New York residents, add local sales tax for subscriptions. (For subscriptions outside the United States, add $7.00 for shipping via surface mail or $25.00 for air mail. Orders *must be prepaid* in U.S. dollars by check drawn on a U.S. bank or charged to VISA, MasterCard, or American Express.)

SINGLE COPIES cost $25.00 plus shipping (see below) when payment accompanies order. California, New Jersey, New York, and Washington, D.C., residents, please include appropriate sales tax. Canadian residents, add GST and any local taxes. Billed orders will be charged shipping and handling. No billed shipments to post office boxes. (Orders from outside the United States *must be prepaid* in U.S. dollars by check drawn on a U.S. bank or charged to VISA, MasterCard, or American Express.)

SHIPPING (SINGLE COPIES ONLY): $30.00 and under, add $5.50; to $50.00, add $6.50; to $75.00, add $7.50; to $100.00, add $9.00; to $150.00, add $10.00.

ALL PRICES are subject to change.

DISCOUNTS FOR QUANTITY ORDERS are available. Please write to the address below for information.

ALL ORDERS must include either the name of an individual or an official purchase order number. Please submit your order as follows:
    Subscriptions: specify series and year subscription is to begin
    Single copies: include individual title code (such as MHS59)

MAIL ALL ORDERS TO:
    Jossey-Bass Publishers
    350 Sansome Street
    San Francisco, California 94104–1342

FOR SUBSCRIPTION SALES OUTSIDE OF THE UNITED STATES, contact any international subscription agency or Jossey-Bass directly.